Amending the
Christian Story

$\mathcal{A}$mending the Christian Story

The Natural Sciences as a Window into
Grounded Faith and Sustainable Living

RON RUDE

RESOURCE *Publications* · Eugene, Oregon

Resource Publications
An Imprint of Wipf and Stock Publishers
199 W. 8th Ave., Suite 3
Eugene, OR 97401

www.wipfandstock.com

PAPERBACK ISBN: 978-1-6667-1862-1
HARDCOVER ISBN: 978-1-6667-1863-8
EBOOK ISBN: 978-1-6667-1864-5

09/24/21

With appreciation for the world's natural scientists
and for the Christian community.
—RON RUDE

Contents

CONTENTS

PART FOUR: THE WAY FORWARD

Prologue

I HAVE LIVED IN sunlight and slogged through alpine sleet. I have touched a dog's nose and held two daughters at birth. I have seen miraculous recoveries, administered CPR as a volunteer EMT, and almost lost my own life in a freak car accident. I have loved the same woman for over forty years and observed up close unimaginable poverty in both body and spirit.

I have been granted a life to live.

Although this life has embodied moments of melancholy and burden, some imposed and others freely assumed, my days have been mostly regenerative.

Admittedly odd to say, I do not care for nighttime. Usually a lighter sleeper, I envy Jesus slumbering through a storm while boating. I hear many a nocturnal coyote, wind rustle, morning-paper delivery, wall creak, and siren. So I love when morning breaks. Even when darkness stays the dawn in wintertime, I get up and am happy. If I were a bird, I would be among the happily chirping.

Along with the air in my lungs and the dins of history pulsating through the ecosystems and cultures within which I abide, I realize more and more how I have been shaped by the Christian community. Old souls, college students, babies held at baptisms. A frustration at times, to be sure, this church community. Nevertheless, it is necessary and mostly on the side of goodness. Whether joined with it in battle, or battling against it from within and without, the church has been my formative companion.

With a deep awareness of my earthiness in body and soul and with an inner joy in God's grace, I now write this love testament. It is for the Christian community, the natural sciences community, and beyond. I have stumbled onto something ancient and new, but mostly unfamiliar. I am convinced my fellow travelers will benefit from what breathes within the perimeters and parameters of this offering. Whether it proves transformative or not, I willingly leave for God.

Ron Rude
ronrude2@gmail.com

Introduction

All is of consequence, including the narratives
we inherit and (a)mend.

MOST CHRISTIAN BOOKS TAKE it as a *given* that Christian theology
has been pretty much figured out. The basics have endured twenty
centuries of rigorous biblical scholarship and theological debate, as
well as the even more erratic filters of numerous cultural, historical,
and technological paradigm shifts. To be sure, various Christian denominations and subgroups will always haggle over nuances—the
word *haggle* might be too tame of a word—but it is assumed that
Christianity's foundations, its historical context, the way Christian
faith is framed, and the basic narrative have hung together quite
well. What is left is simply to learn these truths more faithfully and
to live them out more bravely.

I have been uneasy with this assumption, this "given," in recent years. I do not pretend to be alone in this feeling. My own story
includes serving as an ordained Lutheran pastor (ELCA) for several
decades, including as a campus pastor at the University of Arizona
in Tucson the last seventeen years.

At age eighteen, I went off to college intending to investigate
the humanities. My interests included music, history, religion, psychology, philosophy, and politics. The natural sciences sparked little
curiosity in me.

However, since these college years and my subsequent seminary studies, and even during my early years as a parish pastor, my passions have been steered in a new direction. This is ironic to me. Would you believe that today I find myself delving into the natural sciences—astronomy, geology, evolutionary biology, paleoanthropology, ecology, and other such fields—as much as I do biblical and theological works? In fact, it is within the contours of these scientific fields that I am discovering the more fascinating current window into my evolving faith.

This book is an attempt to articulate a different take on God's story of life and God's story of Jesus. I am especially intrigued by the intersections between Christian theology and Nature's natural sciences. I believe the implications of these soft and hard intersections have a lot to teach our species, including Christians, about faithful and sustainable living.

In this journey of mending and amending the Christian story that I am proposing, I am borrowing from many sources. Among these are the writings of Daniel Quinn, including his monumental work *Ishmael: An Adventure of the Mind and Spirit*. His engagement of the biblical characters of Abel and Cain (Gen 4) is especially helpful, and I will likewise be using these parabolic figures as a "background templet" for describing two very distinct ways of being in God's world. I refer here not to the agricultural vs. animal-husbandry methods of making a living, or even to proper tithing habits, but to something even more contrasting and, I think, more profound. My assertion is this: historic Christianity, shortly after its inception, rapidly regressed into Cain Christianity. That is, in the church's theology and practice, Abel of Nazareth (Jesus) transmuted into Cain of Nazareth (less than Jesus). After laying some necessary groundwork in the beginning chapters, what I mean by this will become clear by chapter 5.

At the time of this writing, we are living with the uncertain effects of a global COVID-19 pandemic. A new reality is upon us, altering not only bank accounts and daily work and play habits, and even anticipated lifespans, but also worldviews. Maybe even theologies, too. Have we reached a tipping point? Could this tipping point be one that has been looming large but unacknowledged right in front of our faces for quite a while?

Added to this is the growing exposure of racism and White-rule structures in the United States and other nations. Lives and institutions, and especially policing protocols, are being turned inside out. We seem to be at a turning point. Could one era be ending and another being birthed?

Of equal weight in the United States is the passing, but not disappearing into obscurity, of the nearly diabolical Trump/Pence era. This brand of conservatism gave voice to and exposed a deep-seated culture within a portion of the American populace that can only be described as distressing. The consequences of this vile underbelly came to a disquieting head in the January 6, 2021 executive-branch terrorist attack against the legislative branch of the US government. Even now there are citizens, some professing a Christian faith, who deem the troubling ideology of this movement to be honorable and worthy of propagation.

Finally, there is ecological well-being, or rather, ecological not-so-well-being. The consequences of generations of ecological irresponsibility, as well as the persistence of continuing entrenched patterns of misbehavior, are crying out for attention. A new paradigm is needed. Action is of the essence.

How did we get here? Where do we go from here?

For many, addressing such challenges will be all about election strategies, new and innovative technologies, medical advancements, and even targeted legislation. This is needed, certainly. However, I detect something deeper going on.

This book suggests what a reframed and recast version of the Christian faith might be able to contribute. It describes what following Jesus could look like were we to set aside all forms of anthropocentricism and dominion-ism. It especially embraces the natural sciences and ecological integrity as foundational. In my view, what is needed is an ecology-theology-*grounded* Christian faith.

Here is a brief tour of the book's contents:

PART ONE examines pivotal moments in the story of the universe, and what Nature's natural sciences are teaching us about God's creation.

PART TWO suggests a recent and consequential mutiny in a species that likes to call itself a primate (primary) and *Homo sapiens* ("wise one").

PART THREE is God's response. What will God do with a species at war with God and with what God holds dear?

PART FOUR summarizes a way forward. It adopts a version of the faith that I am calling "Abel Christianity."

Along the way you will discover footnotes on many pages. Some of these are required citations. However, others also either invite you deeper into the main subject matter of the page or take you into a fascinating (to me) sidebar. My intention is that these footnotes will enhance the more integrated message.

Throughout the book, I try to give full voice to both the pastoral word of God and the prophetic word of God. "Pastoral" refers to God's grace and love for all creation, including humanity. "Prophetic" is used in the biblical sense. The prophetic word in the Bible does not mean predicting the future. A prophet is no clairvoyant. Rather, the prophetic word discerns the present, only with a deeper wisdom than what most are perceiving. With such eyes-wide-open attentiveness to the now, prophetic sensibility sometimes uncovers disturbing realities beneath the shiny (or murky) surface, prompting the prophet to sometimes project likely, though not inevitable, future consequences. But mostly, the prophetic word of God helps us see what is going on right under our noses in our time and place.

"Amending the Christian Story" provides a vehicle for honestly assessing our presence as a species. It offers a road to travel on as we face anew old challenges erupting from our past, tackle the present, and move forward into the future.

Rather than fancying humans as squires of the Earth, distinct from and even above Nature, humans need to learn to live respectfully and deeply with and within the ecosystems and communities of life in God's household. In fact, if we neglect this endeavor, we will be evermore incapable of adequately understanding what God is up to. In other words, it is not so much that we need to better understand what certain passages in the Bible have to say about creation and Nature and ecology as it is that we need to return to and be engaged in Earth's ecosystems and species diversities in order to understand what the Bible (and the Christian faith) has to say about anything.

As we journey together, I pray that you will find in these renderings a truer *version* of God's ancient and vast story of life, and within this larger saga, a more inspired understanding of God's recent story of Jesus. May this offering assist you in unpacking, practicing, and living out more dangerously and courageously a deeper Christian faith for this new time.

PART ONE

Wondrous Universe

Chapter 1

Christianity and Judaism: Infant Religions

WE FORGET THAT CHRISTIANITY, like Judaism, is a new, modern, baby religion. This is something the natural sciences have taught me. These faith systems have been around for only a short time (2,000 years and 3,500 years, respectively). God's actual story is longer and larger.

Although estimates vary a bit, most astronomers, astrophysicists, and mathematicians today calculate the universe's age to be about 13.8 billion years.[1] For people of faith, this is how long (at least) the reign of God has been in business. This is how long the Divinity has been creating, engaging, inspiring, renewing, loving, forgiving, guiding, confronting, challenging, and undergirding all that is, seen and unseen.

Of course, scientifically speaking, the biblical writers were not privy to much of the unseen world. The relatively recent inventions of the microscope and telescope significantly expanded the scope of our knowledge. Since then, numerous additional scientific instruments have enabled us to peer ever more deeply into both outer

1. The "supernova" calculation method puts the age at about 12.5 billion years (plus or minus 0.3). The "cosmic microwave background" (CMB) method puts it at 13.799 billion years (plus or minus 0.021) (Tyson, *Cosmic Queries*, 120).

space and subatomic inner space, detecting dimensions of God's world our ancestors never imagined.[2]

It is impossible to overestimate the extent to which these learnings have altered our perceptions. Worldviews today are fundamentally different from those of Martin Luther and folks of the sixteenth-century Reformation(s) era, as well as from those of our forebears in Bible times. How significant is this? Does it matter that God's universe has existed for 13.8 billion years? Or that Earth, which emerged around nine billion years later, is a relatively new and smallish speck amidst unimaginable vastness? Should this affect how we view God's story of life, and within this ancient and expansive context, God's story of Israel and of Jesus? And might this knowledge alter how we perceive Earth's ecosystems and creatures, including humans?

Earth was formed from remnant dust and debris swirling around the Sun about 4.5 billion years ago. Since the planet orbits the Sun once per year, we can say that Earth has orbited this star about 4.5 billion times.

Around 3.8 billion years ago, the miracle of *life* emerged. How did this happen? What sparked such a wondrous wonder? To date, no one has been able to figure out how non-life becomes life, or how to replicate this process. Single-celled at first, for three billion years tiny life-forms called cyanobacteria not only learned how to live and move and engage with the Creator (in their own way),[3]

2. In the early 1600s CE, Galileo Galilei (1564–1642) and Johannes Kepler (1571–1630) devised refracting telescopes for use in astronomy. In the 1670s, Antonie van Leeuwenhoek (1632–1723), known as the father of microbiology, was among the early microscope inventors and users. With these breakthrough instruments, both the world of smallness and the world of largeness took on startling new meanings. Since then, other complex instruments have been invented to support scientists in a variety of fields, including DNA sequencers, MRIs, the Hubble telescope, the soon-to-be-launched James Webb telescope, seismographs, magnetometers, mass spectrometers, and various particle accelerators and detectors that "see" unseen realities across the electromagnetic spectrum.

3. I find it conceivable that the Creator would interact with all of creation, not just humans. This is a faith statement on my part, not science. However, I find that imagining this to be a possibility does modify my view of Nature and even of God.

they also were engaged in the task of creating Earth's atmosphere and biosphere. These microscopic life-forms were decisive in Earth's budding story.

Sometime later, blue-green algae became the first organisms to become capable of photosynthesis. Photosynthesis is a remarkable process by which light photons traveling a distance of ninety-three million miles through open space from the Sun to the Earth combine with Earth's water and soil and carbon dioxide (CO_2) to produce not only life-giving and regenerative biomass, but also an incredibly useful biproduct called oxygen (O_2). Thank goodness for both features, right?[4]

By about 660 million years ago, these microscopic single-celled life-forms had learned how to cooperate sufficiently to produce another wonder which biologists call "multiple-cell life." This was a huge breakthrough. Notice how long it took for this marvel to work itself out.

Up until about 400 million years ago, all plant and animal life dwelled solely in the oceans. The land masses that make up the states where I have lived (Minnesota, New York, Colorado, and Arizona) were basically sterile. No land life existed. Then, life began to move *ashore*. First fungi and lichens and mosses and ferns, followed by insects and amphibians and invertebrates and eventually, vertebrates. It took about 50 million years for the land to become as verdant as the seas—no easy task. How would sea creatures stay hydrated on land? Could they maintain body support and learn to navigate altered sensations of gravity? Which mechanisms would evolve sufficiently to regulate internal body temperature, help life-forms do sex and reproduction, enable creatures to find and digest food, and allow for the proper recycling of waste? Eggs that require only soft and flexible membranes underwater would now need hard

---

4. Perennials build soil; annuals deplete it. Perennial crops, plants, bushes, and trees convert the sun's energy into rich biomass, working in harmony with and bringing increase to the life-giving cycles of the Earth. This is why industrial farming, a system built almost entirely on annual crops such as corn, wheat, soybeans, sugarcane, and rice because of the greed of industrial agricultural companies—and so dependent today on soil-depleting and polluting chemical fertilizers—is degenerative. Such farming is contrary to Earth's wise patterns. Perennials caress God's creation; annuals diminish it.

shells to survive on land. Over time, evolving life-forms adapted and learned new and complex strategies for living. Some insects even learned how to fly by about 325 million years ago.

Reptiles emerged around three hundred million years before our time. These include three categories: tortoises and turtles, crocodiles and alligators, and lizards and snakes. Reptiles are mostly four-footed, live on land, and lay hard-shelled eggs on land. A few snakes and lizards even hatch their hard-shelled eggs inside their bodies and then give live birth to live babies through the birth canal out into the outside world.

Dinosaurs emerged around the same time, large and small and everything in between. Some were vegetarian, while others were carnivores or omnivores. Because of the arrangement of bones and muscles in their rib cages, many were slow moving and lumbering, especially the larger creatures. But others developed powerful lung and leg systems that produced great capacities for strength, endurance, and speed. There were airborne dinosaurs too, some able to glide from high places to low places, and others, like the *Pterosaurs,* capable of actual self-powered flight.

Small mammals followed about one hundred million years later, living concurrently with many dinosaur species. As the name suggests, mammals, both female and male, have mammary glands (the male mammary gland is not as developed). They also do live births (females), have external scrotums (males), are warm-blooded, sport backbones, require oxygen from the atmosphere, and— unlike fish or reptiles—are clothed in hair or fur.

∾

It is important to note that the trajectory of life in God's household has not unfolded without minor and major upheavals. In fact, there have been four major near-death experiences for our planet's biosphere—439 million years ago (86 percent life extinction), 364 million years ago (75 percent life extinction), 251 million years ago (96 percent life extinction; all of today's life-forms evolved from the remaining 4 percent), and 214 million years ago (50 percent life extinction).

Then, sixty-five million years ago a fifth near-death event occurred. A six-mile-wide asteroid broke through Earth's protective magnetic and atmospheric shields and crashed headlong into our future home. With a force of 10^{14} tons of TNT, this celestial mass of rock and ice struck the terrestrial in the region of the Yucatán Peninsula of eastern Mexico. Massive fires broke out across the planet and tons and tons of dirt, debris, and sulfur fluttered high into the atmosphere, creating a blockage of life-sustaining sunlight. Food sources were decimated. In addition, carbon dioxide (CO_2) molecules, many of which had been safely sequestered in the limestone deposits of the ocean floor, were thrust skyward. Attacking local, regional, and global ecosystems, massive quantities of unleashed toxins spread around the globe, triggering the extinction of 76 percent of all life-forms on Earth. This asteroid, along with perhaps some "perfect-storm" major volcanic action and disease spread, brought a relatively sudden end to the dinosaur era. Just about all these animals went extinct, except for a few that survived and eventually evolved into creatures that today are called "birds."[5]

About sixty million years ago, some of the small mammals that survived the asteroid collision were able to discover new niches. This enabled them to adapt, diversify, and grow larger. Today's renditions include mammals such as cattle, elephants, wolves, felines, bears, deer, and many others.

One mammal, the bat, even learned how to fly. There are about 1,400 species of bat in the world, with wingspans ranging from five inches to over five feet. Weights range from that of a penny to 2.6 lb. Unlike birds with flight-assisting feathers, mammalian bats employ stretched skin for their wings. It is true that some mammals

5. Spiking CO_2 levels caused by human pollution have today's scientists from multiple fields—including astronomy, climatology, oceanography, phenology (seasonal changes), evolutionary biology, botany, geology, Arctic studies, tree-ring research, biochemistry, forestry, zoology, hydrology, paleoanthropology (humanity's predecessor species), medicine, epidemiology (disease), neuroscience—very alarmed. The biosphere recovers eventually from these catastrophic elevations, but it takes centuries or thousands of years.

are called "flying opossum" and "flying squirrel." However, these creatures, like the Asian colugo and the African palm civet, can only glide from high places to low. They cannot perform true self-powered flight.

About fifty million years ago, something counterintuitive occurred. Several land-mammal species began to evolve *back* into the ocean, becoming aquatic and dependent on marine ecosystems for their existence. Whales, dolphins, porpoises, manatees, and dugongs evolved from predecessor land mammals. Like all mammals, they are warm-blooded, do live births, have mammary glands, grow fur or hair, have backbones, and must come up for air. Even those whales that can stay underwater for up to an hour eventually must surface for a gulp of atmosphere. Currently they are fully aquatic and can no longer survive on land.

Sea lions and seals, on the other hand, are semi-aquatic. These mammals spend most of their time swimming in and under water, though always needing to come up for air. They also come onto land for mating, breeding, and molting. Sea lions have a bone structure in their front flippers that enables them to sort of "walk" on land. The physiology of seals, however, lacks this bone structure. On land, seals can only roll their fat around, or "blubber slug."

Polar bears and sea otters are also semi-aquatic mammals, though unlike the others, they feed on land and can navigate both the waters and terra firma quite skillfully.

Approximately 5,400 species of mammals still exist today. These include 331 *marsupials*, such as the kangaroo, opossum, bandicoot, koala bear, and hairy-nosed wombat. Marsupials give birth to tiny babies the size of a peanut who climb back into the mother's pouch for the remainder of gestation. Opossums are the only marsupials in the Americas.

Monotremes make up a small but curious group. These include the Australian platypus and four species of anteaters. Oddly, these mammals lay eggs. And although they have lactating mammary glands (hence they are mammals), because they have no nipples or breasts, milk for their young just oozes through the mother's skin and fur, which the babies then lick and slurp.

Finally, there are 5,080 known *placentals*. These include rodents, such as mice, chipmunks, and guinea pigs, and larger land creatures such as wildebeests, giraffes, humans, armadillos, apes, and bears. The presence of a placenta enables the exchange of nutrients and waste products between the mother and the baby in her womb for the full gestation period. This is the largest group of mammals, of which humans are members.

By the way, Jesus lived as a hairy, back-boned, warm-blooded, placental mammal of the species *Homo sapiens*.

Primates arrived on the scene by about thirty million years before our time. Currently, this category includes mammals such as lemurs, tarsiers, humans *(hominids)*, monkeys, and apes. Of the 250 primates remaining today, seventy-five reside only in the country of Brazil.

∿

So, what about *hominids*?

Evidence from numerous scientific fields suggests that humanity's immediate predecessor species—*Australopithecus, Homo habilis, Homo erectus*—were here about 3–4 million years ago, along with about thirteen other cousins, all of whom have become extinct.[6] Our own species, *Homo sapiens*, has been around for nearly 300,000 years, including a more modern version with certain language abilities and ranges of expression and symbolic thinking for about 90,000 years. This is a relatively short time in God's story.

Like other plants and animals, humans have always migrated. We began spreading around the continent of Africa early on, and probably started to move beyond it around 150,000 years ago. This occurred in periodic waves. There is evidence of reaching the Fertile Crescent (Iraq and parts of Syria and Turkey) and southern Asia 80,000 years ago, Australasia and Oceania 65,000 years ago,

---

6. Human-predecessor species discovered so far include *Sabelanthropos tchadensis; Kenyanthropus platyops*; several forms of *Australopithecus*, including *afarensis, africanus, garbi, aethiopicus, sediba, robustus, boisei*; and several *Homo* species including *habilis, georgicus, erectus, ergaster, antecessor, heidelbergensis, neanderthalensis,* and *floresiensis*.

southern Europe and the Iberian Peninsula 60,000 years ago, China 40,000 years ago, and into the Americas 15,000 to 22,000 years ago.[7] By the way, the self-designation *Homo sapiens* means "wise one." It is a name we have alleged for ourselves. Do you ever wonder about this term given our record of misbehavior as a species—warfare, greed, pollution, self-destructive and other-destructive tendencies? Do you think the rest of the community of life, or even God, concurs? We will be exploring the implications of this question in subsequent chapters.[8]

This chapter has provided a very quick survey of the history of the universe and story of life on Earth. Obviously, this synopsis is brief and limited. The scholarly world of scientific journals and peer-reviewed research is extremely intricate. Also, as hypotheses and theories are continuously tested and new evidence found, conclusions rightfully get altered. But I have tried as a curious layperson to gather from professional natural scientists what appear to be the most widely accepted current understandings and dating figures, gladly acknowledging that more research will always be fine-tuning these numbers. Below is a timeline of the universe listing major crossroads in this wondrous story:

Timeline of the Universe

13,800,000,000 years ago   universe begins

4,600,000,000   Sun emerges, followed by planets

3,800,000,000   single-cell life (prokaryotes, cells without nuclei)

7. Scientists track waves of human migration by examining bone fossils and gene-pool markers (mitochondrial genome for females, Y chromosomes for males); archeological evidence and sedimentary-deposit layers; linguistic/language analysis and tool comparisons; and the spread of viruses that are only carried by humans (such as hepatitis 6), bacterium pathogens like *Helicobacter pylori* (common in stomach ulcers), and certain species of lice.

8. We have also included our species under the heading of "primates," which means "primary." Is this an accurate designation or a pretentious and portentous embellishment? What are the larger implications of how one answers this question?

2,700,000,000	photosynthesis
2,300,000,000	oxygen increase from algae
1,750,000,000	single-cell life (eukaryotes, cells with nuclei)
1,300,000,000	cellular reproduction
660,000,000	multiple-celled life emerges (some scientists say 1.2 billion years ago)
543,000,000	Cambrian explosion; burst of life diversity
425,000,000	trilobites, brachiopods, cephalopods, reef systems
395,000,000	sea life moves onto land
325,000,000	insects first take flight
295,000,000	dinosaurs and reptiles
200,000,000	supercontinent Pangaea begins to break apart
195,000,000	small mammals with mammary glands, backbones, live births, fur or hair
140,000,000	fruit-bearing plants
125,000,000	marsupials (kangaroos, koalas, opossum)
65,000,000	asteroid collision and dinosaur extinctions
60,000,000	larger mammals
50,000,000	several land mammals evolve back into ocean (whale, dolphin, manatee, sea lion, seal, sea otter)
35,000,000	felines
30,000,000	primates
5,500,000	formation of Grand Canyon begins
4,000,000	predecessor hominid species (*Australopithecus, Homo habilis, Homo Erectus,* and thirteen others)
3,300,000	early evidence of tool use among hominids
2,600,000	twenty-three sequential cycles of ice ages begin; lakes and rivers form

2,500,000	predecessor hominid species use tools to hunt, prepare food, construct shelter
1,900,000	bison in North America
790,000	early evidence of domesticated fire in hearths of predecessor hominids
780,000	*Homo erectus* migration out of Africa
400,000	first evidence of constructed shelters
300,000	*Homo sapiens*
120,000	Neanderthal *Homo sapiens*
77,000	early art evidence
90,000	modern *Homo sapiens sapiens*
40,000	evidence of sea travel by humans in Australia
36,000	evidence of cave paintings, figurines, bone carvings, burial of dead
35,000	Neanderthals die out; only *Homo sapiens* continue
16,000	humans in North and South America
14,000	Great Lakes form from receding ice age
12,000	agriculture/domesticated animals become commodified
10,000	*Cain's* worldview encroaching
5,500	writing invented
3,500	emerging roots of Israel
2,000 years ago	Christianity begins

Hopefully, it has become apparent why I made the statement at the beginning of chapter 1 that Judaism and Christianity are modern, new, baby religions. Their roots go back only a few years—3,500 and 2,000 years, respectively. The above dating figures are the best approximations to date, but of course are always subject to refinements as new scientific evidence is found and models devised. But do you think this tells us anything significant about God and God's story? Does it provide a revealing perspective about our relatively smallish place and humble role as human beings, one species among many in an incredibly ancient, large, and diverse household?

∾

Reflection Questions

1. The invention of microscopes and telescopes provided the first step in revolutionizing perceptions of the kind of world we live in. What pluses and dangers accompany our letting the natural sciences alter and amend our understanding of God's story of life, and within this context, God's story of Jesus?
2. Is it accurate to call our species *Homo sapiens* ("wise one")?
3. Have you ever considered how new, modern, and recent the religions of Judaism and Christianity are?
4. What surprised you about the Timeline of the Universe?

0   THEORY

     INTERPRETATION

2   WISE MAN   (NO -ONE
                     WHO
                     KNOWS

3   Y

4   10,000

Chapter 2

It's a *Tov, Tov* World

ONE OF THE DELIGHTFUL insights from the biblical storytellers in Genesis 1 is that the Creator considers this universe to be *tov*. This word in Hebrew means "good." As God creates space and time, stars and galaxies, planets and moons, oceans and mountains, atoms and microbes, plant life and animal life (including humans), creeping and crawling insects, and gloriously soaring birds of the air, it is all declared by God to be good, very good. *Tov*. The biblical storytellers excitedly splash this word throughout Genesis 1 to describe Eden (vv. 4, 10, 18, 21, 25, and 31).

It is important to understand that *tov* does not mean "perfect." There never was a time of perfection. There never was an Eden paradise or utopia. Certainly, the natural sciences know this. However, the storytellers in Genesis 1 also know this. Actually, the idea of a blissful paradise of perfection is a much-later Greek and Roman construct that mistakenly, by many Christians and others, got imposed *backward* in time onto this earlier Hebrew concept. Eden was good, but not perfect, according to natural history and according to the Genesis writers. There never was a utopia-like Garden of Eden.[1]

So, if not paradise, what does *tov* (good) mean?

To be sure, *tov* means healthy, sparkling waters and stately, towering trees. It means colorful sunsets and flowers bursting forth

---

1. The Greek word *ou-topos* literally means "no place." By definition, "no place" has never existed.

through melting snow at springtime. It means babies born and relationships of love sustained.

Tov also means thunderstorms, seasonal changes, fungi,[2] beaver dams, owls, and earthquakes. Earthquakes? Yes. Earth is a quaking planet. Earth's crust is made up of giant tectonic plates stretching across vast regions which are always on the move. These plates range in thickness from three miles at the bottom of several deep ocean trenches to fifty miles thick under portions of several continents. Fueled by powerful thermal and magnetic forces in the Earth's rotating, solid-iron inner core and super-hot liquid iron and nickel outer core, and by the near-molten mantle, these tectonic plates constantly slide (or float) around, traveling approximately one to four inches per year. When enough pressure builds, they lunge or snap. This is an earthquake or tremor. These powerful forces are part of a colossal subduction-*downward* and magma-emersion-*upward* circulation system. Earthen materials and chemicals are constantly interacting with systems deep within the Earth, as well as with the biosphere and energies from the Sun. It is part of what makes our home an alive, stirred-up, excited, and excitable planet. In fact, without earthquakes, some geologists believe life probably would not have taken root here.[3]

Tov means snow and ice, uplift and erosion, lightning, phytoplankton, photosynthesis, and hurricanes. Yes, hurricanes not only help distribute the accumulated hot air around the equator belt to other parts of the globe, they also help to counter regional drought systems and to cross-pollinate life-forms between oceans, continents, islands, and atolls. Obviously, if a hurricane (or earthquake) hits me or my town, it is a bad thing. As global citizens, we need to

2. Fungi include creatures such as mildews, mushrooms, moulds, and yeasts. They bring us diseases like athlete's foot, toenail fungus, Dutch Elm disease, and potato blight, but also the wonders of cheese, beer, and yogurt. More than one million species of fungi are estimated to populate the Earth.

3. Geologists Harry Hess (1906–69) and Robert S. Diez (1914–95) developed the theory of tectonic plates in the early 1960s. Because the inner core rotates slightly faster than the rest of the Earth, a huge magnetic dynamo is generated. This magnetic field protects the Earth from catastrophic asteroids and sun radiation. It also helps move the tectonic plates to bring about earthquakes.

faithfully help one another through such catastrophes. But on the larger scale, God has made a *tov* world with hurricanes, for good reasons.[4]

Tov means condensation, conductivity, meteor showers, decomposition, and bacteria. Our bodies contain trillions of cells of bacteria. They are in us, on us, and all around us. Bacterial microbes travel in and out of our bodies constantly, even into our bloodstream and cells, by means of the air we breathe, the food we eat, and things we touch. Yes, if my immune system is compromised and my body gets out of balance, some bacteria can bring on temporary sickness and even disease. But bacteria are just organisms trying to find a place to live and raise a family—like us. In fact, if we were to have the bacteria from our bodies and Earth's biosphere removed, we would die instantly. Bacteria are life-sustaining. They are necessary residents in God's *tov* household.

Tov means volcanic eruptions, sex and reproduction, gravity, tides, youth, middle age, old age, viruses, forest fires, life, and death. Death? Yes, what if nothing died? What if every member of every species that has ever lived still lived? What would this planet be like? We think it is crowded now. But without the reality of death, think of how many Gila woodpeckers there would be? Or beluga whales, Chilean mesquite trees, spotted salamanders, cicadas, and *Homo sapiens*? Such a scenario is too bizarre even to contemplate.

---

4. Hurricane intensity is measured by wind speed: Category One (74 mph), Category Two (96 mph), Category Three (111 mph), Category Four (131 mph), Category Five (156 mph). In my view, Categories One, Two, and Three are part of God's *tov* world. However, the elevated Category Four and Category Five hurricanes we are seeing today exist because of a disturbing mega-trend of human-caused ocean warming. These calamities are not *tov*. Rather, they are the result of greedy behaviors and sinful ideologies and theologies of wealthy nations, including the United States. Alarmingly, mainstream conservatives in the United States (religious, political, economic, media) are doing everything in their power to sabotage efforts to address this ominous warming of the oceans. The seas are the Earth's lungs. Abuse of these lungs is causing deep, systemic climate changes. This unintentional and intentional irresponsibility needs to cease and desist, and more responsible minds and hearts need to prevail.

For good reason, the Creator has woven death into the fabric of life.[5]

Speaking of our species, it took about three hundred thousand years for Earth's human population to reach 500 million. This occurred around 1500 CE. Over the next mere four hundred years the human population tripled, reaching 1.5 billion by 1900 CE. Then, during the next sixty years it doubled to 3 billion. Yikes. In the nearly six decades since President Kennedy's assassination in 1963, Earth's human population has more than doubled again, rising to 7.9 billion in 2021. Future calculations predict 10 billion by 2050, and 14 billion or more by the end of the twenty-first century. One has to wonder whether the community of life in God's household can endure this many of us, and if we can endure this many of ourselves.

High birth rates are only part of the problem, however. As a nation, residents of the United States of America devour approximately seven times our share of the world's resources. We also spew seven times our share of the world's biosphere-damaging pollutants. What does this mean? If our current US population is 330 million, this means that our nation's resource drain and negative ecological impact is equivalent to a nation with a population of over 2.3 billion people. These numbers are certainly troubling; but what if there was no death?

Many traditional Christian theologies (and even biblical writers, like Saint Paul) presume the existence of a time of Eden perfection in the historical past. According to this view, when Adam and Eve sinned, sin infected not only humanity, but Nature too. They would argue that earthly natural phenomena such tornados, viruses, cancer, a bear eating a deer for her noon meal, floods, mosquitoes, pestilence, mortality, and even astronomical events such as asteroids crashing into planets, supernova exploding, galaxies colliding,

---

5. Of the multitudes of species that have existed on Earth, 99.9 percent are now extinct. Humans will be extinct one day also. Is there something instructive about acknowledging this reality? Does it provide perspective? Does it compel greater ethical attentiveness as a species and as individuals? Why do you think some would say yes to this question, and others no? Is there an appropriate answer for Christians and other people of faith?

and stars dying are all the consequence of human sin. This view says that God's creation was perfect until humans sinned. Then it became deficient. Now the whole creation needs to be overhauled. There needs to be a new creation, a new heaven and a new Earth. They would then see the Jesus event as a cosmic and universal intervention by God sent to repair and redeem not just humanity, but also the whole Earth, solar system, galaxy, and universe.

I propose something quite different. An Eden paradise never existed. God's world, instead, is *tov*. Yes, humanity needs healing. And yes, those regions of God's *tov* biosphere on Earth currently being degraded by human irresponsibility need to be checked, restored, and rebalanced. But the whole Earth, solar system, galaxy, and universe are not deficient. They are not in need of overhaul, renovation, or saving. They are *tov*; and *tov* is good enough for God. For good reason, God has created a *tov* world that is good, and God's *tov* universe will always include life and death.[6]

☙

Reflection Questions

1. Were you taught that there was an Eden paradise somewhere and sometime in the past? Is such a notion essential to the Christian story?
2. What teachings about death did you receive from your faith tradition?
3. What surprises you about the kind of world God has made? Is *tov* good enough for you?

good + reliable   uncertain

6. Here I disagree with the great Jesuit theologian Pierre Teilhard de Chardin (1881–1955), who believed the whole universe is currently partial and is evolving (actually, being drawn forward by Christ) toward a final omega point of fulfillment and consummation. No, it is *tov*. And *tov* is just fine in God's eyes.

I also disagree with Daniel Erlander's subtitle in his wonderful book *Manna and Mercy: A Brief History of God's Unfolding Promise to Mend the Entire Universe*. The entire universe does not need mending. It is *tov*. Furthermore, it is arrogant to believe that the sin of one species (humans) on one tiny speck of a planet in one tiny corner of a galaxy amidst a trillion other galaxies put the whole universe in jeopardy.

Chapter 3

God's Word (Voice) in Two Sources

As stated in chapter 1, the Creator's wondrous venture has been going on for a long time, at least 13.8 billion years. There is even something called *multi-universe theory* which posits the existence of additional universes besides our own. These may occur sequentially—that is, a universe expanding and contracting and then seeding a new, next-in-line universe to expand and contract—or concurrently, with many universes operating at the same time. We will never know. However, the immensity of this theoretical possibility is beyond staggering.[1]

Obviously ancient, God's universe is also vast. This is an understatement. Stars and galaxies are enormous, the distances between nearly unfathomable. To put this into perspective, the nearest star/sun/solar system to ours, Proxima Centauri, is 4.2 light-years away.[2] This is approximately 25 trillion miles distant from my doorstep in

---

1. Until recently, astronomers and physicists believed the universe would expand to a certain point and then gravitational forces would cause it to reverse course and contract back into a singularity (or nothingness). Lately, the consensus seems to be that the universe will expand and expand until it all peters out some trillions of years into the future.

2. A light-year refers to the distance light can travel in a vacuum in a year's time going the speed of light, which is 186,282 miles per second (or about 670 million mph). Our fastest space rockets are comparatively very slow, going only about 40,000 mph.

Tucson, Arizona. The planet Mars is only about 35.8 million miles away. It will take 9 months for a personed spacecraft to travel to this neighboring rock going the fastest our rockets can fly. (It took only 3 days to travel the 240,000 miles to the moon.) Doing the math, if it takes 9 months to travel to Mars, at similar speeds how long will it take to get to the Proxima Centauri sun/star/solar system? Answer: not 9 months or 9 years or even 900 years, but over 30,000 years—one way!

With this in mind, will humans ever travel beyond our solar system to our nearest neighboring sun/star/solar system? The word "unlikely" may even be an overstatement. I am mostly in favor of all astronomy research and space exploration. It is incredibly open-ended and exciting, and NASA scientists and others have come such a long way. However—forgive me for stepping on toes here—*Star Trek* is not humanity's future. The rigors of space distances will make such transport impossible. Our human physicality is the limiting factor also. Even after only a year's time in space, there are issues of space-radiation damage, optic-nerve impairment, significant muscle and bone atrophy (even with rigorous in-flight exercise), and unknown physical and psychosomatic challenges to the human body and mind. We are physical creatures. Along with this, unpredictable solar flares and crashing micro-meteors can cripple any spacecraft instantaneously. And while sterile and sanitized oxygen (O_2) can be put in a tank and brought along in a spacecraft, how will it be possible to bring along a robust biosphere—that is, a host of alive, microbial-filled, self-reproducing, multi-layered chemical and biological ecosystems? Such complex systems (beyond the oxygenated air we breathe) are necessary for extended life processes.

My apologies also to *Star Wars* fans. Humans will not be flying off to other stars/suns/solar systems to fight spectacular, entertaining wars. And *Battlestar Galactica* (notice the war-glorification themes)? The closest spiral galaxy to our Milky Way galaxy, Andromeda, is 2.5 million light-years away. Space travel there will require not 30,000 years of speeding rocket flight, but millions of years to reach any suns/stars/solar systems in that galaxy—again, one way. Science fiction is loads of fun, and, as I have said, I am in favor of astronomy research and all the peaceful space exploration we can accomplish. We should keep doing it. However, reality tells me that this Earth is the only biosphere that Earth's creatures, including humans, will ever be invited to inhabit.[3]

By the way, besides the Milky Way galaxy with its roughly two hundred billion suns/stars/solar systems, astronomers now estimate that there are over a trillion additional galaxies beyond ours. Some of these complex assemblies contain several hundred thousand stars/suns/solar systems, and others as many as three trillion.[4]

But here is something equally stunning. Not only may deep outer space be infinitely vast, but deep inner space may also be unending. As microscopes and other scientific instruments gain power into the infinitesimal world of tininess, we find that the inner space world of atoms, protons, neutrons, electrons, quarks, bosons, photons, neutrinos, and more may be equally limitless.

All this is to say that God has a big job. God's *primary mission* of tending to this evolving story is longsighted and large.

The history of this primary mission is also being recorded. Where? Where do we find the record of the Creator's primary mission, of God's long-running, creating, and tending "voice"? This voice/word is recorded in the "earthen vessels" of stardust and atoms, fossilized remains and geological layers, tree rings and polar icecaps, chemical markers and biomarkers, and the DNA, outward culture, and internal history of every living and extinct ecosystem and species.

I like to think of this record as a kind of "scripture." It is not hard for me to imagine every ecosystem and species in the universe, including our own species, "reading" these scriptures *in their own*

3. The biosphere is seven miles down into the ground beneath our feet, and seven miles up into the skies. Think of the skin on an apple. Earth's precious and thin life skin of soil and atmosphere is the only zone on Earth wherein life lives.

4. Astrophysicist Neil deGrasse Tyson reminds us that expeditions of exploration historically were undertaken and funded primarily for economic (the Americas) or military (US vs. Soviet Space Race) reasons. It is quite likely that going farther into space will have little or no economic or military benefit. Also, such endeavors will be enormously expensive and will drain natural resources. Tyson wonders if voters and their elected representatives will be willing to fund research and space exploration for the sheer joy and challenge of it. He hopes so.

language. Such tactile and intuitive understandings are necessary for a species to survive and thrive and keep evolving.

What does this record tell us? Among other things, this ever-expanding testimony recorded in Nature reminds us that humans have been on Earth for a tiny fraction of time. In fact, doing the math, we have been here for only about 1/15,000 of the time life has flourished on this third rock from the Sun. Furthermore, we are just one out of about twenty million other species who have been invited to take up residence in the Creator's household on this planet.[5]

So here I propose a radical idea: the Divinity is making use of two "scriptures."

For Lutherans and other heirs of the sixteenth-century Reformation(s), the notion of *sola scriptura* (the Bible alone) is something we have consistently tried to hang on to. *Sola scriptura,* rightly so in my opinion, was meant to diminish the stifling over-emphasis in the medieval church on dubious traditions such as priestly celibacy, indulgences, and papal authority, and to instead elevate the importance of the Bible as the more reliable source of God's voice/word. However, I am suggesting here that there are actually two scriptures—Nature and Bible. In my view, they are equally authoritative and equally instructive. They equally convey God's voice and word.

How does this play out? The Creator's first and primary mission is recorded in the Creator's first and primary scripture—that is, in the writings of stardust and atoms, geological layers and fossilized remains, tree rings and polar icecaps, chemical markers and biomarkers, and the DNA of all ecosystems and living things. God has been embedding this story for at least 13.8 billion years and continues to do so today. Christians and others will do well to be up to speed on these testimonies.

---

5. As John 14:2 says, "In the Creator's house there are many dwelling places" (my paraphrase). The Creator's household is wherever the reign of God is, including heaven, Earth, Mars, Proxima Centauri, the Milky Way, and the entire universe. Again, this is a faith statement on my part. On planet Earth there are twenty million dwelling places, one each for the twenty million species that call this place home. The species *Homo sapiens* gets one of these rooms. This raises an important question: What kind of housemates are we being?

Then there is also a more recent collection of writings, or scriptures, called the Bible. This voice/word of God, spoken through the messy lives of very human and contextualized writers, is much more recent—only about three thousand years old. Although several centuries of oral traditions likely circulated before these words found the more preserving safety of print, they are still quite recent. These writings allude to but explain very little about God's primary mission or about God's primary scriptures. While all of God's creation reads the scriptures of Nature, obviously these secondary scriptures, the Bible, are only read by one species, *Homo sapiens*. It is for and about us. Why do you think this is? I will be exploring this question in chapter 10.

As with the record called the Bible, the record called Nature is also an "earthen vessel." It contains God's voice and word, but it does not equal God's voice and word.

Saint Paul in 2 Cor 4:7 reminds us that the "treasure" (God's message) is always in "earthen vessels" (clay jars, cracked pots) (RSV). Why? Because it needs to be "made clear that this extraordinary power belongs to God and does not come from us" (NRSV), or anything else that is created.

Martin Luther provides another helpful analogy when he describes the sixty-six books of the Bible as a manger. The manger holds Jesus. Go to the manger and we will find the Christ. But we will also find wood, straw, and manure. Do not mistake the wood, straw, and manure for the Christ. The Christ, the Word of God, does not equal the earthen vessel that holds it. To think like this is idolatry, or bibliolatry.

So, Lutherans and other Christians do not believe that the Bible is the "pure" word of God per se, or that the Bible equals God, or equals God's word. Rather, we have the incarnate (enfleshed) word of God in written form conveyed through the wonder, messiness, and imperfection of fleshy human lives and earthy context. We do not believe the Bible is the word of God. Rather, we believe it holds (or contains) the word of God. This word needs to be mined (as one mines rock to find gold). Hence, the need for biblical scholarship and interpretation. Therefore, to attach the word "inerrancy" to the Bible is a silly and inappropriate imposition.

The scripture called Nature is the same. It does not equal God or God's word. But in, with, under, and through this "earthen vessel," God will speak truth. Christians need to pay attention to this voice/word in Nature's natural sciences as much as to God's voice/word being spoken through the earthen vessel called the Bible.

∾

Reflection Questions

1. Do you accept the view that there never was a perfect Eden paradise?
2. Why do you think God's universe is so big?
3. Does humanity's relative infancy and smallish-ness as a species inspire you or make you feel unimportant? Does it bring hope and comfort to your soul, or disquiet?
4. Besides the example of hurricanes, can you think of other examples of *tov* events which are thrown out of balance by human misbehavior (sin)?   INSIDE OR OUT
5. What if *Star Trek* is not humanity's future? What if Earth is the only planet we get? How does this affect your personal morality and ethics in the public sphere?
6. Are the two "scriptures" of Nature and Bible equal in significance for you? Should one outweigh the other?
7. Does it matter whether one thinks God interacts with all ecosystems and creatures and not just humans? Why do you think so many humans try to make themselves loom large (hubris)?

Community - not just humans
word made flesh

Chapter 4

Creationism, Intelligent Design, God of the Gaps, Evolution

BEFORE INTRODUCING WHAT I am calling God's *secondary mission,* a holy undertaking that focuses on humanity and Israel and Jesus and is recorded in the secondary scriptures of the Bible, I have one more thing to say about God's primary mission and primary scriptures. There are four main approaches to understanding God's universe that Christians and others tend to use. Some of these approaches warrant greater credibility, others less. The approaches are as follows:

- *Creationism,* the least credible in my view, claims that God created the universe, including Earth, in six days. In fact, they say, this occurred about six thousand years ago. In this view, every species is created "as is." There is no evolution. Adherents claim God made prairie dogs *prairie dogs,* cacti *cacti,* turtles *turtles,* dolphins *dolphins,* hummingbirds *hummingbirds,* and humans *humans*—that is, "as is." There is no such thing as predecessor species. Because of the short six-thousand-year time span, not only were dinosaurs around when humans began roaming the Earth according to this view, but God also intentionally deposited fossil remains along various geological layers and sent photons traveling the speed of light into space just to throw scientists off and test our faith in the Bible. People who hold this view often reject just about everything Nature's natural sciences are teaching us, though ironically, they seem to eagerly embrace *scientism*. Scientism is humanity's misuse of scientific engineering to dominate Nature. I will be saying more about this in chapter 6.[1]

- There is also *intelligent design*. In this view, the universe could have been created "as is" in six days about six thousand years ago, or it could have been created over billions of years through evolution. Either way is fine. However, in this view, some form of cosmic intelligence stands behind it all and is directing it all. This intelligence could be a religiously oriented divinity (God), or even a more scientifically creative galactic brain system ("may the force be with you"). Either way, there is order, intelligence, and design that guides everything. Some kind of "Being" is in charge.

- *God of the gaps* is another approach. This perspective recognizes several major knowledge gaps within the natural sciences, mysteries that numerous fields have yet to figure out or replicate. For example, how did nothing become something? Perhaps this is where God comes in.

There is also the gap between how large things function in the universe (black holes, galaxies, stars, planets) and how tiny things function (molecules, atoms, protons, electrons, neutrons, electrons, quarks, leptons, bosons, photons, neutrinos).

---

1. In the year 1654, Archbishop James Ussher of the Church of Ireland "calculated" that the universe began a little over six thousand years ago. By computing biblical numbers and years and guessing at lengths of generations, and adding them all together, he determined that the first day of creation was October 23, 4004 BCE.

The current fundamentalist Creation Museum in Kentucky, and its nearby theme park called Ark Encounter, both embrace this view. Established by the apologetic group Answers in Genesis (AIG), these venues find ways to fit Adam and Eve, Cain and Abel, dinosaurs, plate tectonics, diamond creation, fossil fuels, Noah's Ark, the Ice Ages, the Grand Canyon, and even the light-year vastness of the universe into a six-thousand-year time frame. Most Christian groups, including my own, do not regard this pseudo-science as science, this pseudo-history as history, or this pseudo-biblical scholarship as biblical scholarship.

The contradictory laws governing these two worlds appear to be irreconcilable. No one has found a unifying theory of everything yet. Could God be the great unifier? Another gap concerns how nonlife became life. This was a huge jump. Could the essential spark and connector be God? There is also the expansion from single-cell life to multiple-cell life, which, as I mentioned in chapter 1, took approximately three billion years to accomplish. Did God facilitate this giant leap? Finally, there is the intriguing question of "consciousness." An assortment of species, including humans, seem to have consciousness. What is this wonder? A physicality? Chemistry? Electricity? A complex phenomenon relating to bosons and subatomic fields? Spirit? Soul? Something else? No one knows. In the God-of-the-gaps theory, a God figure is invoked to fill these gaps.

- Finally, there is the notion of *evolution*. In an ever-changing universe, life-forms constantly evolve to "fit in" with ever-changing changes. In this view, there may be a God, or there may not be. However, the science of evolving life does not really require a God figure or higher intelligence for it to work. The universe is not a clock that needs a supreme clockmaker to manufacture and keep winding it. Instead, with evolution, life bubbles up from below. Simple life-forms evolve into other life-forms and even more complex life-forms through random mutations and natural selection.[2]

2. Another view among some religious groups is that although the evidence for evolution in other species is overwhelming, humans are exempt from this process. They claim we are exceptional and special, created "as is."

Also, some religions hold the view that although humans may have initially evolved from predecessor species like everyone else, at some point in history we received a soul from God. This makes us, and only us, separate and unique. I disagree with these distinctions.

Which of these four approaches make the most sense to you? Personally, I find the evidence for life evolving in an ever-changing universe compelling. To me, these deep and complex processes are wondrous and inspiring. What an amazing world this is. Even the little I have come to understand as a layperson who loves Nature's natural sciences fills me with gratitude and curiosity. However, as a person of Christian faith, I also have to confess that I believe in a creating and tending God who is in, with, under, behind, and over it all. This is a faith statement on my part, not science. I cannot prove this theoretically, mathematically, or in a laboratory. I am not even sure what I mean by this outlook. And certainly, it is correct to say that the science of evolving life does not require a God figure for evolution as currently understood to function. However, this fascinating mixture of evolution and intelligent design seems to make the most sense to me at this point in my developing understanding. This does not mean that intelligent design should be taught as science. No. It is a faith matter.

It is noteworthy that without academically knowing what today we call the natural sciences, the biblical psalmist nevertheless understood viscerally and intuitively and poetically how remarkable God's creation is. All of Nature can resonate with these inspired words:

> Praise the LORD from the earth,
> you sea monsters and all deeps,
> fire and hail, snow and frost,
> stormy wind fulfilling his command.
> Mountains and all hills,
> fruit trees and all cedars.
> Wild animals and all cattle,
> creeping things and flying birds.
> Kings of the earth and all peoples,
> princes and rulers of the earth.
> Young men and women alike,
> old and young together.
> Let them praise the name of the LORD.
> (Ps 148:7–13a NRSV)

∾

Reflection Questions

1. Which approach or combination of approaches for you most accurately shines a light into God's story—creationism, intelligent design, God of the gaps, or evolution?

2. Are there consequences to how one answers this question? Does a person's worldview affect values and behaviors?

3. How viscerally and intuitively did our human forebearers, including some of those in the Bible, grasp what today we moderns know only through the natural sciences?

PART TWO

Amiss and Awry

Chapter 5

Humanity's Recent Regression

GOD'S PRIMARY MISSION OF creating and sustaining a *tov* world is longstanding and immense. This story is told in the scriptures of Nature, which all ecosystems and creatures, including humans, "read" in their own "language."

In contrast, the religions of Judaism and Christianity are young (3,500 years and 2,000 years, respectively). Which raises several questions: Why did these religions surface when they did? What prompted their emergence (or revelation)? Why are they mostly addressed to humans, and about humans?

The marvel of evolving life has been occurring on Earth for 3.8 billion years, and even the species *Homo sapiens* has been around for about 300,000 years. If you are a person who believes in God, as I do, the burning question is: Why did God decide to act in this manner *then*? What prompted the Creator to rouse Judaism's and Christianity's seed beginnings at these specific historical moments? On the other hand, if you are a person who has a hard time accepting the existence of a divine being and feel that all religions, including Judaism and Christianity, are human constructs imaginatively arising out of human circumstances and cultures, your question might be better put this way: What was going on in humanity's inner and outer world during those times that may have prompted individuals and communities in specific geographical locales to devise these religions—these ways of being and these ways of understanding the Earth, themselves, the universe, and God?

These are intriguing questions to me, and I do not have a surefire answer. Sorry. Such things may never be truly known. However, I do have a theory (hypothesis, supposition, possibility, thesis) which I will be exploring over the course of the next several chapters. This thesis has been fermenting in my heart and soul for a while now, sparking, among other things, a restlessness and reticence toward current versions of Christian theology. My premise is grounded in an ecology-theology perception of God's story, and it is inspiring my journey in search of a *truer* Christianity. After all these centuries, it is no doubt arrogant on my part to be seeking a truer version of the Christian faith, and to be wanting a mending and amending of how we understand and talk about God's story of life and God's story of Jesus. But I believe the versions we have inherited are in certain ways inadequate to the daunting trials facing us.[1]

Generations of ecological irresponsibility by Christians and others are reshaping Earth's biosphere. This relentless recklessness will increasingly factor into future Nature-damaging and human-society-degrading incidents of climate volatility, new disease outbreaks, refugee migrations, freshwater scarcity, soil degradation, species extinctions, and wars. We as a species, including those of us in the Christian community, need to dig deeper.

1. I use the word "version" intentionally. God's story of life and God's story of Jesus consist of what "is." Only the Divinity knows this actual story. Such complete knowledge is far beyond the purview of any created creature, including humans. So, in lieu of possessing what is actually actual, we possess versions. A version is just that—an estimation, an approximation, a version. It does not equal the actual. The Bible is an assortment of versions of God's story of life and God's story of Jesus. So are various versions of historic and contemporary Christianity, the natural sciences, various religions, art, literature, philosophy, commerce, politics, and culture. All these versions have much to teach, and obviously some approximations reside closer to the hub of truth than do others. But all are approximations to be embraced with studied humility.

So, here is what I am proposing. I believe that Judaism and Christianity, addressed to and about the human creature, emerged very recently as a *response* to a recent and significant paradigm shift within our species. This paradigm shift has had far-reaching negative effects. These negative effects are present today, and escalating. What was the nature of this shift? What were these religions responding to? My thought is this: after approximately 300,000 years of living in relatively honorable and complementary ways with and within God's community of life under the permeating reign of God, and after 300,000 years of evolving slowly but surely like all other creatures, recently—perhaps 6,000 or 8,000 or 10,000 years ago—our species started to backslide. We began to de-evolve, to decline, to *regress*. Maybe not so much in terms of "smartness"—we are plenty smart. But in terms of "intelligence," and even more ominously, in terms of "wisdom." Here is how I am using these words:

- *Smartness* is the ability to manipulate information, people, and events; literally, to get what one wants. There are plenty of smart people in the world, some honorable and others nefarious.

- *Intelligence*, on the other hand, is less common. Intelligence is the ability to enter multiple layers of complexity. It embraces nuance. It thinks and acts beyond instant gratification. An intelligent person (or community or nation) is capable of standing on the outside and can both comprehend and fairly articulate viewpoints and perspectives other than their own.

- *Wisdom* is the rarest character trait of all, and the most important. Wisdom perceives the bigger picture and the longer term. It strives for the common good and the well-being of all God's creation. Wisdom is capable of appreciating perspectives beyond the merely human. Most importantly, wisdom is grounded in ethics. As such, the search for what is moral and ethical is not relegated to the afterthought or sidebar elective invoked in the service of convenience. Rather it is *the* piercing center and circumference of every individual and collective thought, word, and deed. Wisdom knows and acts on bigger truths.

35

I am suggesting that while "smartness" continues to increase (wax) within our species, the trajectories of "intelligence" and "wisdom" have been diminishing (waning) for several millennia.

I am fully aware that this thesis goes against the grain of how many civilizations perceive themselves, including Western civilization, and including American culture. We like to think of ourselves as intelligent and wise creatures, and that our levels of intelligence and wisdom have kept pace with any ascending smartness we may have achieved. In fact, many of us like to think of ourselves as progressing, individually and as a species. We even ascribed to ourselves the self-designation *Homo sapiens*, which, as noted earlier, means "wise one." But here are a few examples of what I mean by regression:

- It takes a lot of smartness to make a Coca Cola commercial—that is, to associate a concoction of mostly unhealthy chemicals and water with a person's ability to discover purpose in life, happiness, and maybe even true love. Juxtaposed with images of joyful fulfillment, Coca Cola slogans tout: "It's the real thing . . . Coke adds life . . . pure as sunlight . . . things go better with Coke." To be sure, these commercials are nothing short of brilliant, and a lot of crafty smarts (and money) goes into accomplishing each ad's ambition. But consider this: Doesn't the fact that we actually *fall* for this trick demonstrate a rather significant level of *low* intelligence?[2]

- Another, more serious example. Currently, the governments and military forces of nine nations have armed themselves with weapons of mass destruction—nuclear, chemical, and biological. The nine offending nations are the United States (1945), Russia (1949), UK (1952), France (1962), China (1964), India (1974), Pakistan (1980s), North Korea (2006), and Israel (which refuses to confirm or deny its status to the world community).

2. I remember the predaceous marketing smartness employed by the Philipp Morris Company when they came up with the novel idea of a designer cigarette expressly for women. They called these smokes "Virginia Slims." Their ads during my teen years exploited the growing women's equality movement with this catchy tune: "You've come a long way, baby. To get where you've got to today. You've got your own cigarette now, baby. You've come a long, long way" (Marilyn, "Cigarette Ads of 1972," para. 1). Ugh.

At this moment, these nine nations wield vast arsenals of ecosystem-degrading and species-destroying WMD's aimed at God's creation, including humanity. This means that these countries have policies in place that declare to God and God's world that "if our lifestyle is threatened, we will not only commit devastation and mass murder against those who threaten us, we will also generate genocide, ecocide, and biocide against large swaths of God's household for generations to come." These nations have decided that "if necessary," they are willing to vitiate Earth's life-giving and life-sustaining biosphere.

Surely it takes a lot of smartness to make even one WMD, let alone a doomsday arsenal. But the fact that these nations have empowered mere military generals to obey orders from mere politicians to launch such demonic technologies, and that citizens in these countries are so numbed that we hardly even think about it—well, doesn't it seem as though both intelligence and wisdom, let alone faithfulness, ethics, and honor, have vacated the souls of a portion of humanity? It is not difficult to imagine God's anguish at such depravity.

- During the past one hundred years, there has been a dramatic and perverse philosophical/theological/ethical shift within the human soul vis-à-vis our animal cousins. As Israeli historian Yuval Noah Harari vividly describes in his book *Sapiens: A Brief History of Humankind*, "farm animals stopped being viewed as living creatures . . . and instead came to be treated as machines." Farm animals are today being "mass-produced in factory-like facilities, their bodies shaped in accordance with industrial needs." For example, "egg-laying hens . . . feel strong urges to scout their environment, forage and peck around, determine social hierarchies, build nests and groom themselves. But the egg industry often locks the hens inside tiny coops," in cages "so small that hens are often unable even to flap their wings or stand fully erect" for the entirety of their lives.[3]

---

3 Harari, *Sapiens*, 342.

In similar fashion, amply intelligent and inquisitive mammals such as pigs are forced to spend their whole lives locked in industrialized cages that "routinely confine nursing sows inside such small crates that they are literally unable to turn around (not to mention walk or forage). The sows are kept in these crates day and night for four weeks after giving birth. Their offspring are then taken away to be fattened up and the sows are impregnated with the next litter of piglets."[4]

Furthermore, "many dairy cows live almost all their allotted years inside a small enclosure; standing, sitting and sleeping in their own urine and excrement. They receive a measure of food, hormones and medications from one set of machines, and get milked every few hours by another set of machines."[5] These comparatively sanitized descriptions are just the tip of the iceberg.[6]

- Finally, natural scientists understand that each year a couple dozen of the approximately twenty million species in God's *tov* household on Earth naturally go extinct. As stated before, the marvelous phenomenon of evolving life is not so much a matter of "survival of the fittest" as it is survival of those species that "fit in." For many reasons, certain species begin to no longer fit in, and they die out.[7]

4. Harari, *Sapiens*, 342.

5. Harari, *Sapiens*, 342.

6. Also, Joel Salatin is an organic farmer, owner of Polyface Farms in Virginia (www.polyfacefarms.com), and writer of several books, including *The Marvelous Pigness of Pigs*. He is not a vegetarian. He knows that animals eating other animals is part of God's *tov* world. In addition to the planting and growing of vegetable crops, his multigenerational family farm also breeds and raises chickens, pigs, cattle, and turkeys for human consumption. However, he believes every animal has a right to be who they are and to live their life in a suitably healthy environment . . . up until the day they are butchered. To rob them of this is not only criminal, but also a sin against Nature, against decency, against God, and against Christian faithfulness. I agree.

7. Charles Darwin (1809–82, born the same day and year as Abraham Lincoln), did not introduce the term "survival of the fittest." An English contemporary, Herbert Spencer (1820–1903), coined this phrase and applied it to economic and military antics. This misnomer became known as social Darwinism.

However, because of misbehavior by major portions of the human family, currently more than sixty species *per day* are disappearing. This is according to the Field Museum of Natural History in Chicago, the Center for Biological Diversity (www.biologicaldiversity.org), National Geographic, and many other scientific sources. Is there something amiss about a species that would foster such annihilations? And speaking as a Christian, since Christians are doing as much damage as anyone, is there something awry in my own community's understanding and practice of the Christian faith and story? I believe so. Hence, this book.

These are just a few of the many examples of human advancement in terms of smartness accompanied by a palpable regression in the arenas of intelligence and wisdom.

Reflection Questions

1. Discusses the distinctions between smartness, intelligence, and wisdom.
2. Can you think of other examples where smarts are in play but intelligence and wisdom (including ethics) are lacking?
3. In what ways have you felt Christianity's historic and current versions of God's story to be inadequate?
4. Does the Christian story itself need mending and amending? Does the Bible need mending and amending? Is it okay to determine that certain biblical passages are inadequate or even wrong in what they teach?

CIVILIZATION

Chapter 6

Man Is the Measure? Not

So, what is at the heart of this regression? Returning to the questions I raised at the start of chapter 5, what conditions precipitated the recent advent of both Judaism and Christianity?[1]

Answer: at the heart of this regression is a newly emerging worldview/narrative/myth.

After approximately three hundred thousand years of *Homo sapiens* living, a new worldview began showing up within our species. This began occurring approximately six thousand to ten thousand years ago. Over time, it gained traction. It took root and spread. Because of its fundamentally violent essence, it quickly infiltrated, compromised, and eventually dominated neighboring cultures. In our day, this worldview infects nearly every human society and nation on the planet. In fact, it has surpassed all other worldviews and become the dominant narrative of our species. This worldview (or narrative, or myth) is the championed (or acquiesced) foundational narrative of just about every political speech, every textbook, every newscast, every parental instruction, every graduation address, and most sermons.

The newfound worldview is this: Humans Rule.

---

1. Similar factors regarding humanity's regression may have also sparked the emergence of other modern religions, such as Hinduism (2300 BCE), Buddhism (500 BCE), Taoism (350 BCE), and Islam (610 CE).

Rather than seeing humanity as embedded with and within the multilayered ecosystems and species diversities in God's household under the permeating reign of God, which is intelligence and wisdom, this worldview began to position the human creature as separate. This worldview catapulted humans to the head of the class, the front of the line, and the "top of the toppest." Instead of embracing a theological narrative that lifts up all of Nature, including humanity—we have a right to be here too—into God's grace granted as a gift for the sake of all, this new and devastating narrative claimed the following:

Earth belongs to humans.

Humans rule.

Everything is for and about *us.*

The concept of narrative (or worldview, story, myth) is instructive. Families embody distinct narratives about themselves that play out through peculiar character traits, behaviors, and even vulnerabilities over several generations. Cultures, tribes, and nations also have myths about how they came to be and who they are now. More often than is realized, these myths shape a nation's character, political and economic decisions, news reporting, elections, and even wars. Even individual species have internal and visceral narratives that are unique to their own DNA and to their distinctive biological and communal traits. We can think of intricate groupings such as pods (whales), packs (wolves), hives (bees), coveys (quail), shoals (sea horses), cetes (badgers), cauldrons (bats), gangs (buffalos), quivers (cobra), courts (kangaroos), convocations (eagles), dazzles (zebras), shivers (sharks), skulks (fox), troops (monkeys), bale (turtles), rookeries (penguins), congregations (alligators), skeins (geese), cackles (hyena), clowders (cats), consortiums (crabs), hoards (hamsters), thunders (hippos), creams (turkeys), and nurseries (raccoons), to name a few. Primeval biological and cultural narratives shape who we are. They fashion the contours of where we fit in, life's daily and ultimate purposes, our relationships to other species, and how we behave.

Over a series of generations, this regressed narrative—Earth belongs to humans—has gone on to permeate numerous human cultures near and far, wreaking various degrees of disconnectedness and resultant havoc. Specifically, in a relatively short time, the human species vis-à-vis the rest of God's household has moved from being mostly *eco*centric, to being predominantly *ego*centric. In this "I-centered" arrangement humans have come to see themselves as separate *from*, superior *to*, the reason *for*, and the rulers *of* all that is, seen and unseen. There is us—and then there is the environment. We actually talk this way. In reality, however, there is only the environment—which includes us. Through our language and behavior, we imagine humans as distinct from everything else and destined to be in charge. Through countless ways and means, we daily declare entitlement to every square foot of land and sea and air on the planet. Some even think this entitlement extends into the solar system and beyond.

The Greek philosopher Protagoras of Abdera (circa 490–420 BCE) articulated this disconnectedness in his famous dictum: "Man is the measure of all things."[2] We are the yardstick and the plum line, the judge and appraiser. We determine what is of value and what is not.

The British philosopher and statesman Sir Francis Bacon (1561–1626) asserted the same worldview with different wording:

> Man, if we look to final causes, may be regarded as the center of the world, insomuch that if man were taken away from the world, the rest would seem to be all astray, without aim or purpose.[3]

Really?

In the late 1700s, John Jay (1745–1829) emerged as one of America's founders. He helped negotiate the Treaty of Paris (1783), authored five of the eighty-five *Federalist Papers* (1788), and served as the first Chief Justice of the United States Supreme Court (1789–95). Reflecting the values of his White contemporaries, he characterized the American continent this way:

2. Martínez, "Man is the Measure."

3. Bacon, *Wisdom of the Ancients*, chap. XXVI, para. 3.

Extensive wildernesses, now scarcely known or exposed, remain yet to be cultivated, and vast lakes and rivers whose waters have for ages rolled in silence and obscurity to the oceans, are yet to hear the din of industry and become subservient to commerce and boast villas and gilded spires and spacious cities rising on their banks.[4]

John Quincy Adams (1767–1848) was an experienced statesman and courageous opponent of slavery (one of America's original crimes/sins). He served as our sixth president (1825–29). Subsequently, he served as a respected congressman from Massachusetts in the US House of Representatives (1830–48). Unfortunately, "Old Man Eloquent" also championed the serviceable fiction of this new narrative. In debates among White men over whether to commandeer Native lands in the Pacific Northwest and consign these regions to American hegemony, he argued that the young nation was fulfilling God's command to "subdue the earth." He considered the wilderness to be wasted if it merely remained "hunting grounds for the buffalos, braves, and savages of the desert." In his view, White America was ordained to turn the wilds into a cultured garden and "no longer prolong the domination of the buffalo and bear."[5]

Even more so today, this narrative—Humans Rule—permeates our discourse and policies. The state of Arizona's consideration of future water usage presumes human entitlement, stating, "Key to this Roadmap is the understanding that the 'water needs' and 'health' of an ecosystem are defined within the context of human priorities."[6] Unfortunately, current water-usage standards adhere to the following priorities. First place: the non-conservationist-minded American consumer (and the industries that support them). Second place: displaced Native Americans living on reservations. Third place: the needs of Nature's ecosystems and communities of life.[7]

4. "Treaty of Paris," sec. "Part 3: Peace."

5. Quoted in Wheelan, *Mr. Adam's Last Crusade*, 226. From correspondence between John Quincy Adams and a friend in 1846.

6. Mott Lacroix, *Roadmap*, iv.

7. Salty seas account for 97 percent of Earth's water. Salinity rates vary. The Dead Sea (which borders Jordan, the Palestinian West Bank, and Israel) is 25 percent salt; the Great Salt Lake in Utah is 17 percent salt; the Mediterranean

What if these priorities were reversed? What if firstly we made sure that the complex ecosystems and species diversities of a given region were safeguarded? These are the essentials to all of life, including human well-being. Once health and sustainable footing are upheld, what if secondly the United States finally did right by Native communities and served their needs and priorities? And thirdly, with what is left, what if responsible and mature leaders in government, business, religious groups, and media helped the rest of the American populace engage in practicable principles of conservation? Do you think such a values-inspired prioritization could be our guiding light going forward? Could it replace the current demeaning values of extravagance, planned obsolescence, dominion-ism over Nature, and mindless wastefulness?

What is this relatively new narrative (or worldview, or myth) called?

"Human exceptionalism" is a commonly used term. Human exceptionalism believes that humans are *the* exceptional, stand-out species. Not only are we greatest in importance according to this view, but our very presence provides meaning and purpose to all ecosystems and life-forms. They are here to serve us. We are singularly special.

Another term is "anthropocentrism." *Anthropos* is the Greek word for "human." There is also "anthropo-narcissism" and even "human entitlement."

Sea is 4–6 percent salt; and the Atlantic and Pacific oceans are 2–5 percent salt. Only 3 percent of Earth's water is fresh water. Two-thirds of this amount is required for maintaining ice caps, permafrost, and glaciers, or lies too far underground to access. Therefore, only 1 percent of Earth's H_2O is available fresh water. This precious remnant must sustain all land life, including humans, and all creatures who inhabit lakes and rivers.

What about desalinization? Unfortunately, desalinating salt water into fresh water has serious negative consequences. This process burns enormous amounts of energy and involves intake forces that seriously degrade marine life. Furthermore, the discharge of salty brine (tailings) has proven to be too concentrated and toxic to be put back into the ocean. And either piling it or burying it on land will cause significant harm to biomass, freshwater aquifers, and soil.

A friend of mine, invoking this implied level of exaggerated self-importance, perceptively calls the narrative "diva theology." All these terminologies describe quite accurately the regressed narrative that I am talking about. However, the term that makes the most sense to me is *human-ism.* This term best describes the outsized worldview/myth/narrative/storyline that this book is challenging, a storyline that ranks the species *Homo sapiens* as primary. Human-ism asserts that humans are foremost, top dog, at the center of the universe, the one species above all others.[8]

Human-ism's creed and accompanying behavior is this: Nature is a rough jungle—a dangerous, deficient, defiant, disorderly enemy. It is wild and needs to be tamed, broken and needs fixing, inept and needs to be controlled. Nature is mostly just a wayward, underdeveloped, and underperforming wasteland until visited upon by humans for "development."

Furthermore, in this view, those 13.8 billion years prior to our recent arrival were just preparing the cosmos for us. Our vocation now is to conquer it, rule it, use it as desired, and discard the rest as expendable. Furthermore, we should not stop our quest to command land, sea, sky, weather, wildlife, bacteria, genes, artic icecaps, and every cubic inch of this biosphere until this holy mission is fulfilled and creation lies bleeding at our feet—until we have transformed both God and Nature into *our* image. Human-ism is humanity's incandescent claim before God and before all the other ecosystems and species on this planet that we are not only special and entitled, but that we are also intrinsically and ontologically superior.[9]

8. I understand that "humanism" is a term normally used in contrast to isms that invoke a deity figure. Here I am using "human-ism" to summarize a worldview that positions the needs and wants of *Homo sapiens* as paramount.

9. I recently passed the local Humane Society in Tucson and wondered how this name was chosen to represent an organization dedicated to optimal kindness toward animals. On so many levels, humans are a ruthless predator species not only toward our own species (war), but toward many animals as well (industrial food companies). Rather than using humanity as the standard for honorable behavior, maybe it would be better to call it "Animal Society" or "Wildlife Society."

Reflection Questions

1. Do you agree that the notion that "Humans Rule" and that "it is all about us" is the dominant narrative in our species today? Do you think it has always been this way, or, as I am suggesting, that this is a recent aberration?

2. Unless significant cross-species communication becomes possible in the future we cannot know this for sure, but do you think other creatures besides humans have culture and psychology and sociology and religion and educational systems? Does one's answer to this question affect one's values, worldview, and behavior toward other creatures?

3. Can you think of better terminology than *human-ism* to describe an anthropocentric worldview?

4. Discuss the quotes by Protagoras, Francis Bacon, John Jay, and John Quincy Adams.

5. What do you think of the idea of reversing our water priorities?

Chapter 7

Implications of Decline

AS THIS NEW NARRATIVE took root just a few thousand years ago, intelligence and wisdom began to wane, diminishing the capacity of eyes to see and ears to hear.

- For example, *economics*, which should be the wise management of the whole household, or "eco" (*oikoi* in Greek), constantly regresses into mere human-ism. The responsibility of wisely working with and within the *oikoi* erodes into a relentless quest to acquire more and more accoutrements for ourselves, much of it nonsense, and much of it wasteful and polluting.

- *Politics* should be the art and science of seeking the common good. This also regresses into human-ism, becoming a tedious and droning warfare of words, conquests, maneuverings, guns, and missiles.

- *Academia* gets trapped in the ideology, too. I am always amazed at the care professors and students must take to make sure their research and grant proposals are justified in terms of profitability and comfort for humans. If they are not, their research is often underfunded or rebuffed as irrelevant.

- The *natural sciences* make up a principal method for learning about God's world. The goal should be to plumb Nature's wisdom, let these lessons sink in, and then produce goods and services and lifestyles that are wholesome and complementary to these embedded patterns. Unfortunately, this too regresses into human-ism, or what I call *scientism*. Scientism, as opposed to science, stands over and against Nature. Scientism seeks to overpower and subdue. Scientism treats God's world as a thing, an "it," a mere commodity. Scientism's forces daily wage warfare against the beloved ecosystems and life communities that make up God's household, and it sees this warfare as a necessary and inspired accomplishment. Some even render it humanity's divinely ordained destiny. As alluded to earlier, while today's mainstream conservatives (political, economic, religious, media) are endeavoring to distort or debunk learnings from the natural sciences, it fits their ideology to wholeheartedly champion the Nature-dominating tentacles of scientism.

- Finally, even *Christianity* in my view has regressed into human-ism. I know this is a presumptuous and sweeping accusation to make, but I make it anyway. Christianity's versions of God's story of life and God's story of Jesus, including those of my own Lutheran tradition, have become greatly anthropocentric. Christianity in many ways has fallen into just another form of I-centeredness, which is the very definition of sin. Downgrading God's primary and secondary missions, we have shrunk a grand and comprehensive story into a mere diminutive melodrama about how much we think God gushes over *us*.

The implications of this new narrative have been far-reaching. In positioning humanity as separate from, superior to, the reason for, and the rulers of the world, it has helped to turn humans into a species doing considerable harm. In the process, we are wedging many of the biosphere's robust patterns out of their natural balance and health.

∾

Reflection Questions

1. Discuss chapter 7. Do you agree that human-ism has also overtaken Christian theology and practice?

2. In addition to economics, politics, academia, scientism, and the Christian faith, have you noticed other arenas wherein human-ism has become the regnant worldview?

Chapter 8

What Does It Mean to Be Human?

So, IF WE ARE not divas as *Homo sapiens*, nor the crown of creation, nor even God's primary obsession, what does it mean to be human? Firstly, we are placental mammals. This means that we have mammary glands, backbones, and fur or hair. We have a placenta and do live births, similarly to elk and cats and whales and sea lions. We are warm-blooded and have external scrotums (males).[1]

The species *Homo sapiens* is also a primate ("primary"), though this self-designation, like the self-designation *Homo sapiens* ("wise one"), is a shaky over-exaggeration in my view. It is sad to observe how readily our species tends to consider itself "legends in our own minds." The category of primate includes monkeys, apes, chimpanzees, tarsiers, humans, lemurs, marmosets, gibbons, and several hundred other species and subspecies, with more being discovered every decade. Primates are always mammals, have five fingers with fingernails (including opposable thumbs), and have skulls containing proportionally larger brains.

What does it mean to be human? Unlike "precocial" animals that can stand, walk, and run and are fairly independent moments after coming out of the womb—javelinas, giraffes, quail, colts, geese, antelope jack rabbits, moose, porcupines—humans are born

---

1. It is believed that male mammals need external scrotums because the inside temperature of a warm-blooded creature is too hot to maintain a healthy sperm count.

"altricial." Naked, blind, and incapable of crawling or walking—like bears, coyotes, squirrels, and all perching birds—humans for many months are wholly dependent on our parent(s). This is because we are born physically and mentally immature. Since hominids began walking on two legs (bipedal) five million years ago, our hips have shrunk. This has narrowed the female birth canal, resulting in human babies requiring smaller, less-developed, and more pliable skulls that can safely navigate a smaller birth passageway. Further development occurs after birth for humans, but for a long while human babies are entirely dependent on others for their survival needs, including food, shelter, warmth, and protection.

Humans also lack the necessary physicality and strength that enables other creatures to accomplish what they do. For example, we cannot live underwater. We cannot fly, let alone backwards and upside down like a hummingbird.[2] We are clumsy on our feet compared to a mountain goat or mule. We have terrible hand-eye coordination compared to that of a squirrel. In terms of speed, we are faster than a sloth but slower than a cheetah—though we are relatively adept at long-distance running. And because our brains are 3 percent of our body weight and require 25 percent of the body's energy while at rest, our muscular strength relative to body size is noticeably less robust than many other creatures.[3]

Furthermore, we cannot change color like some fish, tree toads, or chameleons, or store water like a desert tortoise, saguaro cactus, or Bactrian camel (which can go without water for up to seven months—humans will die without water within a few days). Our eyesight also underachieves when compared to the vision of owls, eagles, and hawks. Bloodhound dogs have smelling capabilities

2. While visiting the Wright Brothers Museum at Kill Devil Hills on North Carolina's Outer Banks, I noticed that the docent liked to claim that the amazing breakthrough of Orville (1871–1948) and Wilbur (1867–1912) in 1903 meant that humans could now fly. Afterwards I reminded him that humans cannot fly, per se. We can build machines that fly, and then we tag along—which is commendable. But we cannot fly and never will have this ability.

3. Pound for pound, not only do animals like chimpanzees and bears have considerably more strength and dexterity than humans, but some ants remarkably can lift and carry up to fifty times their weight.

thirty times more sophisticated than ours, and the sense of smell in grizzly bears is another seven times greater than this. However, what we have is sufficient for being who we are. Our job is to be human beings.[4]

ᴏᴠ

What does the Bible say about our kind? In the earliest creation story in Genesis 2 (written circa 900 BCE), the storytellers write, "Then the LORD God formed the human creature [*adám*] from the soil [*adamáh*] of the ground" (Gen 2:7 my paraphrase). Notice the similarity between these two Hebrew words. Along with other creatures, humans are made from the earthen soil, the dirt. We are earthlings; we are dirt-lings. This is a good thing, not a put-down. It is *tov*.

Furthermore, various fields of biology tell us that each human body, similarly to many Earth creatures, is made up of trillions of cells. However, by number, only about 20 percent of these cells belong to us. This means the other 80 percent of the cells that make up a human body are actually other creatures, such as bacteria, archaea, fungi, viruses, and various microeukaryotic colonizers. So, here is a question: What does it mean to be me when only 20 percent of me is me and I am essentially a *colony* of organisms? Does such biological awareness inform my understanding of who I am and my role in the world? Does it affect my assessment of God's story of life and God's story of Jesus? I have no clue what these biblical storytellers were ultimately trying to say when they portrayed human creatures as made from the soil (earth, dirt), but

4. Swedish botanist, zoologist, and physician Carl Linnaeus (1707–78) came up with one of the early classification systems (taxonomy). This system has expanded over the years as new life-forms have been discovered. Commonly used categories for humans today are: Kingdom—*Animalia;* Phylum—*Cordata;* Class—*Mammalia;* Order—*Primates;* Suborder—*Haplorhini;* Infraorder—*Similiformes;* Family—*Homininae;* Tribe—*Hominini;* Genus— *Homo;* Species—*Homo sapiens.* It should be acknowledged that along with Linnaeus devising this system and even coining the name *Homo sapiens* ("wise one"), he also unfortunately wrought long-term harm to much of humanity by capriciously ranking humans based on race, resulting in numerous diabolical consequences that plague us to this day.

such renderings sure sound similar to what the natural science of evolutionary biology is teaching us.[5]

Consider also the more recent creation parable in Genesis 1 (written circa 500 BCE). Here the storytellers, when describing the sixth day, put into the mouth of "Elohim" (God) these words: "Let *us* make humankind in *our* image" (Gen 1:26, italics added NRSV). This is an interesting bit of dialogue, don't you think? Have you wondered who "us" and "our" refer to? Also, to whom is God speaking? In seminary I learned that it might be the Trinity, although this does not make sense in a Hebrew text. Perhaps it could be a heavenly court of some kind, whatever this means. Or maybe the storytellers are employing a common literary device known as the "royal we."

Here is an alternative thought. Could the storytellers be putting into the mouth of the Deity a conversation between the Deity *and* those lively ecosystems, plants, and animals whom God has already created? "Now, those of you I have already created, listen up. On this afternoon of the sixth day, let us make this next creature, humankind, in *our* image." What does this mean? Could it mean that humans (and all creatures, I would add) are created in the image of God *and* in the image of all other ecosystems and creatures—and that we forget either at our peril? Again, I have no idea what these storytellers are ultimately trying to say, but this sure fits with what the science of evolutionary biology is teaching us also. In fact, most of the DNA found in Earth's other twenty million species is found in the species *Homo sapiens* as well, and vice versa.

What does it mean to be human?

5. Christian tradition at its best tries to maintain this connection. At funerals we affirm soil as life's source and destination with the words "Earth to earth, ashes to ashes, dust to dust." On Ash Wednesday (the beginning of Lent), the imposition of the ashes rite is accompanied by the words "Remember that you are dust, and to dust you shall return." This is not a put-down. Rather, it is a grace-filled reminder of our earthiness and mortality—and, along with other creatures, our dependence on God.

In my view, not every biblical writer gets it right all the time. In trying to answer this question, the storytellers in Genesis 1 also claim for humans "dominion over the fish of the sea, and over the birds of the air, and over the cattle, and over all the wild animals of the earth, and over every creeping thing that creeps upon the earth" (Gen 1:26 NRSV). In making this claim, they were probably unaware of the recentness of our arrival as a species. They also probably did not appreciate that the wider community of life does not need humans to have dominion over them, or even to steward them—although they certainly would appreciate it if we learned how to self-regulate and steward *ourselves*. Other species have been fine without our presence for most of Earth's history, and the Earth will be fine again should we go extinct.

Even the psalmist's insights in Psalm 8 are only partially on target, in my view. The writer starts out wonderfully by exclaiming to God: "When I look at your heavens, the work of your fingers, the moon and the stars that you have established; what are human beings that you are mindful of them, mortals that you care for them?" (Ps 8:3–4 NRSV). The psalmist is rightfully in awe that God would take the time to care for us too. Such attentiveness is amazing and wonderful.

But then the writer descends into an unfortunate muddle, asserting: "You have made humans a little lower than God, and crowned them with glory and honor. You have given them dominion over the works of your hands and put everything under their feet" (Ps 8:5–6 my paraphrase). Hmmm. In my view, these assertions are false. And unfortunately, this worldview has played a huge and tragic role in Western Christianity's regression into humanism, making historic, Reformation(s)-era, and even contemporary Christian theology and practice for the most part pathologically anthropocentric.[6]

6. It is true that sixteenth-century Protestant reformer Martin Luther (1483–1546) expressed some ecological sensibilities, writing, "The created world of nature is charged with the presence of God, who is in, with, and under all things." He also wrote, "If you would really examine a kernel of grain, you would die of wonder" (Martin Luther, *Weimar Ausgabe*, quoted in Bornkamm, *Luther's World*, 182). However, Luther also believed thorns and thistles and mosquitoes and illness and earthquakes and death are the result of humanity's sin, and that

Reflection Questions

1. What new insights into your own humanity does this chapter stir? How do you feel about knowing your body is a colony of other-than-human organisms?
2. Are biblical storytellers ever wrong? About little truths? Big truths? Since they are products of their time, as are we, is it ever okay and even necessary to mend and amend their truths in light of new learnings?
3. Do you agree that Christian theology (including liturgy and hymnody) has become "pathologically anthropocentric?" What might a non-anthropocentric version of God's story of life and God's story of Jesus look like?

---

thunderstorms are caused by demons. He was limited by the medieval world-views of his time and their apparent ignorance of the wider implications of *tov*.

Chapter 9

Cain's Genocide, Ecocide, and Biocide

IT IS CRUCIAL TO understand that the recent Hebrew and Christian Scriptures—that is, the Bible—are not predominantly for and about humanity because we are so special. A portion of our species likes to think that we are God's primary concern and not only more special than all other creatures, but more special than all other creatures *put together.* Many of our kind certainly behave as though this is so. However, this is not the reason for the Bible's focus on humans. Rather, the Bible is for and about us because we are the one species at odds with God and with what God holds dear. We are a species at war with God's primary mission.

Several early stories in the Hebrew Scriptures try to make sense of this regression, this "Fall." There is a sobering parable in Genesis 3 that portrays the human creature as a trespasser. The characters Adam and Eve cross a boundary established by God and attempt to enter God's domain by eating fruit hanging from the forbidden tree of the knowledge of good and evil. What is the point of this parable? In my view, the point is not that there were two actual first human parents named Adam and Eve from whom all other humans are descended, who committed an act of disobedience at a particular moment in history that consigned all of humanity to expulsion from Eden. No, it is a parable. The point also is not that humans have eaten the fruit, had their eyes opened, and become wise, and should now just move forward and learn how to manage this accidental wisdom responsibly. No. Nothing could be further from the truth. We may be able to eat the fruit, but we cannot digest it.

Rather, these biblical storytellers are trying to make sense of something novel and vile happening in their actual time (three thousand years ago) and in their actual locale (the Middle East). What is happening? These storytellers are encountering fellow humans who are professing a new, bizarre, and troubling worldview—that is, anthropocentrism, "diva" theology, human-ism. And they are acting out this narrative. "What's wrong with these folks?" the writers wonder. "Why are these neighbors exhibiting such haughty self-understandings and boorish behaviors? Why do they style themselves as separate from, superior to, the reason for, and the rulers of everything else? Where does such arrogance come from? Could it be they are trespassers? Could it be they have breached God's domain, stolen the goods (the fruit), and now think they are gods, or close to it? Could it be they deem themselves masters? Lords of the garden? Geniuses? Entitled? If so, they are in well over their heads." The storytellers are alarmed by the implications of this new and vile narrative even as they imagine and put into parabolic writing the Creator's sorrow and anger.

A similar scenario of I-centeredness and self-aggrandizement is portrayed in Gen 11:1–9. This story describes a group of human citizens hell-bent on building "towers into the skies." Why are they doing this? Why such ambitious undertakings? Succumbing to illusions of greatness and delusions of grandeur, they clamor "to make a name for [themselves]" (Gen 11:4a NRSV). I-centeredness as individuals, as nations, or as a species is a prime definition of sin in the writings of many Christian theologians. Such behavior distorts the human soul and degrades humanity's relationships with neighbor, Nature, self, and God.[1]

---

1. Of course, "turned in on self," a phrase used by Martin Luther and others to characterize such sin, is not the same as self-care. Self-care is a good thing. Self-care means doing what needs to be done to have a measure of physical, spiritual, emotional, intellectual, and relational health. It is wisdom in action. But "turned in on self" is sin.

Finally, there is the story of Abel and Cain in Gen 4:1–16. The writer Daniel Quinn offers a helpful approach to this story. Using the characters of Abel and Cain as a background template, Quinn suggests that *Abel,* the brother being murdered, represents a narrative and way of living and giving that is pleasing to the LORD (Gen 4:4b). Abel represents the many indigenous cultures that for tens of thousands of years in tens of thousands of cultures and locales around the world lived in relatively complementary ways with God, respectfully embedded with and within the wider community of life. They lived in relative covenant with God's primary mission in their temper, disposition, occupations, and passions.[2]

Cain, on the other hand—the murdering brother and cocky wunderkind—represents all the human ideologies, industries, and deeds of I-centeredness that daily wage war against all that the Deity holds dear, including Nature and including other humans.[3] Daniel Erlander describes Cain's fallenness this way:

> Humans decided to find joy by becoming BIG DEALS. How did humans know if they were big deals? They knew by bossing others around, by piling up stuff, by dominating nature, and by reaching glorious heights of health and

2. To appreciate the scale and array of indigenous cultures around the world, it is notable that a small place like western Canada's Vancouver Island includes peoples such as the Holmaco, Qualicum, Quwutsun, Musqueum, Saanich, Klahoose, SeShalt, Stoilo, Tsawwassan, Coquitlam, Sliammon, Sne-Nay-Mux, Semiahanoo, Esquimult, Comox, Squamish, Tslei-waututh, and Songhees. Arizona's indigenous tribes include the Pascua Yaqui, Quechan, Akimal O'odham, Yuma, Hopi, Chiricahua Apache, Chemeheuri, Tohono O'odham, Shivwits, Navajo, Wlalpai, Maricopa, Pima, Havasupai, Yavapai, Kamia, Cocopah, and Hualapai.

Each culture is unique. Each embodies their own style of hunting and agriculture, philosophy and theology, gender roles and sexual identities, modes of travel and housing, views on child-raising, medicinal applications, worldviews, and values. My argument is that generally, these cultures have seen themselves as viscerally and honorably interwoven with and within Nature's multilayered ecosystems and species diversities—not as separate from, superior to, the reason for, or the rulers of those systems and that diversity.

3. See Quinn, *Ishmael.*

beauty and knowledge. They also knew by having more points than other humans in their scoring systems.[4]

Similar words flow from the biblical prophet Hosea:

> Hear the word of the LORD, O people, for the LORD has an indictment against the inhabitants of the land. There is no faithfulness or loyalty, and no knowledge of God in the land. Swearing, lying, and murder, and stealing and adultery break out; bloodshed follows bloodshed. The land mourns, and all who live in it languish; together with the wild animals and the birds of the air, even the fish of the sea are perishing. (Hos 4:1–3 NRSV)

Many Cain nations, including the United States, have a history of murdering Abel. White America's land theft and cultural/linguistic/bodily genocide against Native families from sea to shining sea is one of White America's three original and continuing crimes/sins (the others being slavery/racism and ecocide/biocide). How could this have happened? Where did the false justification for such wrongdoing come from?

In the 1300s and 1400s CE, governments of White people in Europe (Cain) claimed entitlement to lands belonging to Native peoples in Africa (Abel). In 1452, a document called *Dum Diversas* was issued by Pope Nicholas V, wherein—claiming to represent Jesus Christ—he authorized King Alfonso V of Portugal to "invade, conquer, fight, subjugate the Saracens [Muslims] and pagans, and other infidels and other enemies of Christ."[5] Three years later in his follow-up document *Romanus Pontifex* (1455), he declared that European governments that were Christian had the divine right to "invade, search out, capture, vanquish, and subdue all Saracens and pagans whatsoever" in any discovered lands upon which they could impose their country's flag. In addition, "all moveable and immoveable goods whatsoever" were to be "converted to their use and profit."[6]

---

4. Erlander, *Manna and Mercy*, 2.

5. Nicholas V, *Dum Diversas*, para. 2.

6. Nicholas V, *Romanus Pontifex*, para. 3.

Christopher Columbus (1451–1506) did just this in his four voyages to the Americas (1492–93, 1493–96, 1498–1500, 1502–4). In addition to taking off with tons of stolen natural and human-made "booty," and besides mass murdering thousands of Native families, Columbus and his crews also kidnapped men, women, and children and brought them back to imperial Spain as slaves. In light of Columbus's voyages and the accompanying White-supremacy-laden trip reports, Nicolas's successor Pope Alexander VI instructed Europeans to "civilize" every "savage" they encountered and engage in "Christian dominion and utilization of conquered lands and peoples."[7] This papal bull of 1493 was called *Inter caetera*.

This narrative played out in various forms of colonialism around the world. How did it play out in United States history?

The United States chose to carry on the Doctrine of Discovery and formalized it in 1823. In the landmark case known as Johnson vs. M'Intosh, US Supreme Court Chief Justice John Marshall in effect established the argument that just as so-called "Christian" European nations had assumed ultimate dominion over lands populated by Native peoples in the Age of Discovery, the United States also, by virtue of gaining its independence from Great Britain, had the right to do the same.[8]

Not long after this, Andrew Jackson (1767–1845), a man not only unabashedly proud of his enslavement of Black families but also proud of White America's land theft and terror against Native peoples, said in the first year of his presidency (1829): "By persuasion and force they have been made to retire from river to river and from mountain to mountain, until some of the tribes have become extinct and others are left but remnants to preserve for a while their once terrible names. Surrounded by Whites with their arts of civilization, which by destroying the resources of the savage doom him to weakness and decay."[9]

7. Alexander VI, *Inter caetera*.

8. For a thorough critique of Marshall's arguments and presuppositions, see umass.edu/legal/derrico/marshall_jow.html.

9. Meacham, *American Lion*, 122–23. Acts of land theft and cultural and bodily genocide were carried out by the White US government and military,

Today, as in the Genesis 4 story and in numerous Cain countries around the world, whenever Cain discovers Abel, Cain rises up to kill him, including his culture, language, resources, waterways, land, livelihood, identity, animals for food, and environment. In Abel's world, the Earth belongs to the whole community of life. For Cain, every square inch is and should be available to humans for the taking. In our day, we can see how Cain-ism's industries are lining up right now to exploit the human-caused melting of Earth's polar icecaps. They applaud the opening up of the Arctic and Antarctic regions and look forward to new opportunities for oil and gas drilling, mineral mining, and industrialized fishing.

Abel, of course, has always been a consumer of goods and services too. Within certain ethical perimeters and with a fertile imagination, such human activity is necessary and good for daily living. However, Cain-ism's sin is "entitlement consumerism."[10] Walter Brueggemann describes entitlement consumerism as a worldview whereby one's ability to pay for certain resources entitles one to possess them. If I (or my nation) have the money to extract oil, minerals, or cheap labor, even if these resources reside on or under another nation's land, they are mine. In fact, if anyone tries to keep me from these resources, I have a right to employ economic leverage, political power, bribery, and even police or military force to acquire them. This has been the unembellished basis for many of Cain's wars, including by the United States.

---

winning plaudits from the industries and households of White Americans. Strategies of "laying claim" included surveying and mapping, asserting natural right, asserting divine right, erecting military forts, sending in and then defending White "settlers," and destroying vital native food sources.

Also, they systematically sowed diseases, such as smallpox, measles, and typhus, assassinated Native leadership, employed "divide-and-conquer" strategies, distributed guns and ammunition to both sides in a Native conflict, enslaved Native peoples for free labor or forced sex for US soldiers, and threatened Native leaders into signing detrimental treaties. Inhabitants who fought back were deemed "savages" and inferior in culture, religion, and language. Dehumanization and other forms of shrill "law-and-order" rhetoric have consistently proven to be an effective weapon of conquest for Cain.

10. This is a term Walter Brueggemann has used at various speaking events.

Cain-ism also engages in "totalitarian consumerism," boasting that humanity's desires must always take precedence over Nature's requirements. This is often combined with a near total ignorance of, and even willful disregard for, long-term consequences.

Daniel Quinn's writings again offer a helpful distinction. Abel is a *Leaver*; Cain is a *Taker*. A Leaver, according to Quinn, takes what is truly needed, and leaves the rest.[11] A Taker, on the other hand, is never sated, and knows only how to take and take. A Leaver understands the interconnectedness of the bigger picture and doesn't bristle at limits. A Taker embraces plunder and knows neither when to stop nor how to stop. If something exists, it must be acquired. In fact, according to Cain-ism's stunted ethics, "If I don't take it, someone else will." For Cain, freedom and liberty means that the world belongs to him and he should be free to hunt or fish without limit, pluck up trees and "develop" acreage at will, and graze, mine, burn, drill, and kill without concern.[12]

It is as though Cain sees the world as theater. Humans are the well-paid primary actors. We are the stars whose names light up the marquee. The other twenty million species in God's household are unimportant, unnamed, and among the easily substituted extras. They come and go in anonymity and are hired and fired at will. Their sole function is to serve us and make us shine. The multilayered ecosystems of Nature are the backdrop. These ecosystems provide background scenery, props, lighting, sound, and ambiance. Humans manipulate the stage to serve humanity's story.

Ultimately, what has really happened in our educational systems, mass media, governments, regressed religions (including much of Christianity), households, industries, and businesses is that Cain-ism has gotten the upper hand.[13] This tumbling (mutiny?)

11. Quinn, *Ishmael*, 127.

12. See Quinn, *Ishmael*, 38–39, 126–128, 151–54. See also www.ishmael. org for Daniel Quinn's writings and ideas.

13. In current versions of capitalism, ethics and morality are not major concerns for industries, businesses, or shareholders. This responsibility is relegated to the consumer. The life cycle of every product involves three stages: production, use, disposal. Each stage can be done in the Abel way of intelligence and wisdom, or in the Cain way of smarts. If consumers prefer the Abel way, this is where they will spend their money. The commercial enterprise

into human-centeredness is rendering us evermore disconnected from our human neighbors, from Nature, from our own inner spirits/souls/selves, and from God. The great tragedy is that in countless ways, including in our parenting and educational systems, most of our species has for some time now ceased raising Abel, and has instead focused all energies into raising Cain.

Reflection Questions

1. What do you think of the idea that the Genesis 3 story is attempting to address a recently arrived dynamic (Fall) within the human species?
2. Discuss the Abel and Cain template. Can you think of a better way of differentiating these two very opposing ways of living in God's world?
3. Had you heard of the Doctrine of Discovery ideology? Discuss how it has functioned in America's history and how it is functioning currently.
4. Discuss the concept of Leavers and Takers. How do you see these contrasting approaches playing out in your family system, place of employment, national self-understanding, and personal identity?

---

naturally follows the money. So far, sadly, most consumers continue to declare loudly and clearly by their spending habits that they prefer goods and services that are produced, used, and disposed of under the banner of Cain-ism's values, worldviews, and behaviors, rather than those of Abel.

PART THREE

God's Response

Chapter 10

God's Secondary Mission: Israel

How is God going to fix, or at least manage, a species that has fallen so tragically into this quagmire—as individuals, as a species, and as nations?[14] How will God save God's marvelous household from a creature who presumes entitled ownership?

Very early in the secondary scriptures, the Bible, we have what has been called the "saddest verse in the Bible." In Gen 6:6 the writer cries out, "The LORD was sorry he had made humankind on the earth, and it grieved him to his heart" (NRSV). We do well to let these words sink in. I had not noticed this pivotal verse until recently. It seems the Creator was faced with a dilemma—namely, what to do with a species gone amiss and awry. What would God do? This is a disquieting question. Would God execute punishment? Destroy our species? Allow us to go extinct?

Or would the Creator try to heal us?

---

14. Another favorite weapon in Cain-ism's arsenal is religion-fueled nationalism. We have seen a particularly invidious and insidious form of this jingoism in the Trump-world mantra of "God and Country." True Christian faith, however, maintains different priorities: God first, the well-being of Nature second, the entire human family third, the global body of Christ fourth, and finally—in fifth place—country. God, Nature, humanity, church, country. These priorities transcend all national walls and borders, though they probably do not fit as easily on a bumper sticker. But because of its fundamentally flawed ordering, God-and-country thinking, rhetoric, and behavior sets in motion not just nonsense, but evil.

Apparently, as the inspired biblical writers envisioned it, the Creator gave serious consideration to going down the road of capital punishment. Might *this* be the most appropriate way to solve the problem of human regression? The next verse says: "So the LORD said, 'I will blot out from the earth the humans I have created—people, together with animals and creeping things and birds of the air, for I am sorry I have made them'" (Gen 6:7 NRSV). Chilling, don't you think?

But then God must have thought: "Wait a minute. Can an honorable mother slaughter her brood? Can a loving father butcher his kids? And yikes, why would I want to start behaving like Cain?"

So, instead of destroying us (for the sake of the world?); instead of allowing us to go extinct because we no longer fit into God's holy agenda; and instead even of permitting our continuance on a destructive pathway, apparently—in addition to God's full-time and long-standing primary mission—recently (just a few thousand years ago) God also decided to undertake what I have been calling a secondary mission. The focus of this secondary mission would be to try and heal a very smart but frequently unintelligent and non-wise/non-ethical placental mammal of the species *Homo sapiens*. This mission's goal would be to restore a lost and fractious species to God's larger and more joyful purpose.

This is good news for us, isn't it? But of even greater significance, this is tremendous news for the rest of the community of life in God's household who has suffered so much under the destructive arrogance of Cain-ism's human-ism.

So how will this healing be accomplished? After Gen 6:6, answering this question becomes what the rest of the Bible is all about.[15]

The Hebrew Scriptures portray a very persistent Deity. There is a parable in Gen 6:11–9:28 which involves Nature, the Noah family, and a flood. I use the word "parable" intentionally for two

---

15. It is not unimaginable to me that between the time of Cain's initial mutiny and the nascent seeds of the Israel story several millennia later, God would have undertaken numerous other efforts to try and heal humanity as well.

reasons. First, no department of geology or geosciences in any reputable university in the world would argue that there is scientific evidence of a flood of this magnitude occurring on Earth when humans existed. Annual floods certainly befall various regions across the seven continents, and many constructive and destructive consequences do occur. However, there never was a deluge of such scale that sea levels rose fifteen cubits higher than Mount Ararat in Turkey at 16,946 feet, let alone higher than Sagarmatha (Mount Everest) in Nepal and Tibet at 29,029 feet, as proffered by the storytellers in Gen 7:19–20; 8:4.

But the second reason for thinking this is a parable is of greater weight. If we deem such a catastrophic event as historical and God induced, then we must believe in a God of ecocide/biocide (Nature) and genocide (humans). The parable states that all land creatures, except for a small sample from each species, were drowned. (Evidently ocean fish, ocean mammals, and ocean vegetation were all safe, though freshwater fish, mammals, amphibians, and vegetation would have probably been killed off after being inundated with salty seawater). Furthermore, it states that the entire human race, except for the Noah clan, was wiped out by God. My observation is this: Doesn't such a scenario sound more like the horrific terror of a Nazi death camp like Auschwitz or Buchenwald than the righteousness of the Creator portrayed within and throughout the whole and heart of the Bible?[16]

But if it is a parable, and parables "do not actually happen but are always true"—and usually have a point—what point/truth are

---

16. As a campus pastor, I traveled with college students to the Buchenwald Nazi death camp near Weimar, Germany, the Topography of Terror display in Berlin, the Yad Vashem Holocaust Museum in Jerusalem, and the Holocaust Memorial Museum in Washington, DC. At such sites, one sees all too clearly the destructive depths of Cain-ism's cunning. Besides the 6 million Jews murdered, the German Nazis in WWII bear responsibility for the killings of 23 million Soviet soldiers and citizens, 5 million Poles, 1.5 million Roma (gypsies), 560,000 French, 451,000 British soldiers and civilians, 433,000 American soldiers and civilians, 384,000 Austrians, 270,000 disabled persons, 15,000 LGBTQ persons, 3,000 priests, and thousands of mentally ill individuals.

In our time, Cain is committing a similar holocaust against the life-sustaining soil, water, air, plant life, and animal life of God's beloved household.

these biblical storytellers trying to impart? Certainly the parable wants to portray the scope of God's intimate relationships: "God said to Noah and his sons with him, 'As for me, I am establishing my covenant with you and your descendants after you, *and with every living creature* that is with you, the birds, the domestic animals, and every animal of the Earth with you, as many as came out of the ark'" (Gen 9:9–10, italics added NRSV). God's embrace is comprehensive.

However, the parable also speaks an additional truth, namely this: if we think we can get rid of evil by killing off evil people, we must think again. It doesn't work. Period. Though tried again and again throughout human history, evil keeps rematerializing. Furthermore, the executers of capital punishment always end up also degrading themselves and the society or cause they represent. If this story is historical and God induced, it means that God has regressed too.

How does this parable end? It turns out that Noah, the supposed righteous one, begins acting wickedly almost immediately (Gen 9:20–25). Soon after the ark settles on dry ground, Noah grows a vineyard, ferments a varietal, greedily overindulges, becomes fall-down drunk, and passes out naked in his tent. His son, Ham, who is the father of Canaan, witnesses his father's state of sozzled exposure. But the greater evil is this: when Noah awakens, he is so ashamed of himself and the fact that Ham witnessed his bad behavior that, consistent with Cain-ism's deep psychological brokenness, Noah projects his inner self-loathing *outward* onto Ham. This projection takes the form of a curse inflicted upon Ham's son Canaan and his descendants (Gen 9:24–27). This curse sets in motion a scenario whereby generations of Israelites and others manufacture convenient rationalizations for oppressing and enslaving the Canaanites of this world. Noah declares:

> Cursed be Canaan;
> lowest of slaves shall he be to his brothers. (Gen 9:25 NRSV)

He also says:

> Blessed by the LORD my God be Shem;
> and let Canaan be his slave. (Gen 9:26 NRSV)

This vile misinterpretation infected America's landscape and character as well. White US citizens seized on this story to rationalize their own system of brutal kidnapping, deadly transatlantic transport, destruction of beautiful cultures and languages, and lifetime enslavement of African individuals and families. These mainstream White Americans fantasized that Black Africans were the descendants of Canaan and therefore were rightfully destined to be enslaved. This lie came to a head in 1860 and 1861, when in response to Abraham Lincoln's election to the presidency in 1860, thirteen treasonous legislatures and governors seceded their states from the Union. The states were South Carolina, Mississippi, Florida, Alabama, Georgia, Louisiana, Texas, Virginia, Arkansas, Tennessee, North Carolina, Missouri, and Kentucky.

Many White conservatives today argue that the Civil War from the South's perspective was not about slavery. They even claim that Confederate flags and public monuments honoring Confederate leaders and soldiers are worthy of respect. Lest they get away with such distortions, we note the February 1861 declaration of secession by Texas, which stated: "We hold as undeniable truths that the governments of the various States, and of the Confederacy itself, were established exclusively by the white race, for themselves and their posterity; that the African race had no agency in their establishment; that they were rightfully held and regarded as an inferior and dependent race, and in that condition only could their existence in this country be rendered beneficial or tolerable."[17] The state of Mississippi's pronouncement was similar: "Our position is thoroughly identified with the institution of slavery—the greatest material interest in the world."[18] Speaking on behalf of fellow rebels and in praise of the recently established Confederacy, Alexander H. Stephens, the newly elected Confederate vice president, wrote in March of 1861 that the Confederacy's foundation rests "upon the great truth that the negro is not equal to the white man; that

17. "A Declaration," para. 22. Reading the full document will provide a stark and chilling window into the perversity of thought and distorted rationalizations that lay at the heart of Southern Confederacy values and worldviews. See tsl.texas.gov/ref/abouttx/secession/2feb1861.html.

18. "Mississippi Secession."

slavery—subordination to the superior race—is his natural and normal condition. This, our new government, is the first, in the history of the world, based upon this great physical, philosophical, and moral truth."[19]

It is to the great shame of all Christians that numerous congregants and lay leaders and ordained clergymen and bishops cited biblical texts to defend this evil. One such dishonorable church leader was Rev. Joseph Wilson (1822–1903). He served as a Presbyterian pastor in Augusta, Georgia. He was also the father of Woodrow Wilson (1856–1924), who served two terms as US president from 1913 to 1921. In January of 1861, Rev. Wilson wrote and distributed a lengthy discourse entitled "Mutual Relation of Masters and Slaves as Taught in the Bible." In this treatise, he fashions an educated-sounding ruse for the crime and sin of slavery. Sadly, not only were his White congregants and readers non-astute, but his own hermeneutical immaturity also kept him from realizing that biblical writers could sometimes be errant in their theology and values. Think of how many Black individuals and families were hurt because of such contrived justifications during both the slavery years and since. And think of how many White Americans have had their view of God and God's righteousness temporarily or permanently perverted.[20]

---

19. Quoted in Meacham, *Soul of America*, 54. There are currently over six hundred US monuments erected in public places across the nation that honor Confederate values and leaders. In order to not erase but to truthfully preserve our history's sometimes foul underbelly, these should be dismantled and placed in a yet-to-be-built Smithsonian "Confederacy and White-Supremacy Repository/Museum." Each relocated monument/statue should be accompanied with knowledgeable and transparent commentary describing both the White-supremacist values of the person depicted, as well as the White-supremacist values of the people who erected the monument/statue. There are also one hundred US public schools with names honoring the likes of Robert E. Lee (1807–70) and Jefferson Davis (1808–89). These need to be renamed. Texas and Florida have an annual Confederacy Heroes Day. Tennessee has a Confederacy Decoration Day. Decommissioning such affronts to decency is long overdue.

20. See Rev. Wilson's document at http://www.civilwarcauses.org/revwilson.htm.

Besides clergy, it should also be noted that many physicians likewise betrayed their professional oaths. Among other humiliations, they often

A telling example of how deeply racism dwells in the hearts and myths of White America after the Civil War—and to this day—has to do with *reparations*. When the White crime of official enslavement finally ended, instead of every culpable city, county, and state government, as well as the federal government, focusing all their energies and resources on repaying every ex-slave for every hour of labor stolen, plus damages, White citizens were concerned that the slaveholders were suffering losses. Many efforts were made to reimburse them because their "property" had been taken away. This resulted in ex-slaves soon being abandoned to poverty and other forms of economic and political enslavement. Ensuing hostile measures included voter suppression (systematically being carried out today by today's conservatives); all-White police departments, all-White juries, all-White judges; prioritizing White testimonies over Black testimonies during trials; harassment and brutality by White police; targeted mass incarceration of Black fathers, mothers, daughters, sons, brothers, and sisters while exonerating White citizens who commit the same crimes; post-Civil War sharecropper "slavery" accompanied by White vigilante groups authorized by White sheriffs to terrorize Blacks; "Black Codes"; condoning or failing to prosecute thousands of lynchings of Black men and women by White citizens; redlining; conceiving, enacting, and enforcing Jim Crow segregationist laws; medical experimentation; job discrimination; White rule; White privilege; and more. Such thinking is ensconced in the structures and institutions of much of White America to this day.

Regarding reparations, most White Americans have improperly profited from generations of accrued political and economic advantage, and most Black Americans have been unduly harmed by generations of accrued political and economic disadvantage. Therefore, since this reality was devised, sanctioned, carried out, and protected not by a radical fringe group in the United States but by the federal government itself and by numerous state and local

---

participated in the slavery scheme by assisting slave dealers at "auctions, checking the teeth of human chattel and making them run, leap, and jump to test whatever strength remained after the grueling middle passage" (Chernow, *Alexander Hamilton*, 8).

governments as well, doesn't it make sense that these entities, using US tax dollars, should be responsible for fulfilling the many reparations requirements?

∾

Reflection Questions

1. Discuss the concepts of God's primary and secondary missions and their accompanying scriptures.
2. What do you make of the "saddest verse in the Bible" and God's ultimate decision concerning the human creature?
3. Have you been troubled by Nazi-like behavior attributed to God in the Noah parable?
4. What are your thoughts on restitution/reparations?

Chapter 11

Troubling Deeds and Occurrences

ALONG WITH THE WELCOMED biblical witness of God's efforts to heal Cain, and many narratives that display God's love and persistence, scholars and interpreters continue to anguish over certain disconcerting passages in the Bible. I am referring to episodes of cruelty and massive acts of violence which are often portrayed as occurring under the guise of faithfulness and God's orders. Besides the Noah parable, below are several further examples of behaviors ascribed to God that are troubling:

- Following the idolatrous golden calf incident in Exodus 32, the storytellers report that Moses orders Levi's male offspring to go on a killing spree, instructing: "Thus says the LORD, the God of Israel, 'Put your sword on your side, each of you. Go back and forth from gate to gate throughout the camp, and each of you kill your brother, your friend, and your neighbor'" (Exod 32:27 NRSV). On that day, the sons of Levi abandon all sense of integrity and instead obey Moses' temporary insanity. They murder three thousand Israelites. We can only imagine the long-term grief for each of these families and how this carnage forever distorted their views of the God of Israel. One cannot help but think of the 9/11 terrorists, the European conquistadors, American slaveholders, the January 6, 2021 terrorist attackers on the US Capitol, and the "Manifest Destiny" conceivers and executors who also wrongly considered their brutal deeds to be God ordered.

It is proper that the storytellers would want to expose the seriousness of human sins against God and God's creation, as well as the absolute futility of making anything an idol. Idols include such things as money, power, nation, the Bible (bibliolatry), family, self, fame, Nature, or a golden-calf statue. However, is retributive justice really God's way? The deeper biblical answer is no. Rather than "retributive justice" (punishment and revenge), God's way seems far more concerned with "restorative justice," "distributive justice," and "transformative justice." Restorative justice seeks recuperative healing, especially of severed relationships. Distributive justice is concerned that "all have enough; and none too much" (Daniel Erlander's phrase reflecting this truth in Exod 16:16–21 and 2 Cor 8:10–15).[1] Why? Because to not have enough is deadly. Likewise, to have too much is deadly, certainly to those who are deprived of life's basic needs because of the hoarding of some, but also for the hoarder. Owning too much distorts reality, drives ethics to the margins, and deadens the soul. Furthermore, transformative justice wants to revive and revitalize all involved in the injustice, including both victims and perpetrators, as well as the structures and systems that sanction the injustices.

It may seem uncommon or even heretical for a student of the Bible to say this, but I believe faithfulness sometimes requires us to question whether certain behaviors ascribed to God in the Bible are really of God. This is especially true when they stand in sharp contrast to the deeper heart and whole of God's story of life and God's story of Jesus.

- In Num 11:31–35, when the Israelite wanderers murmur cravings about food shortages, God sends a deadly plague.

- Deut 28:14–68 declares that if Israel disobeys God, God will unleash fevers, ulcers, boils, madness, blindness, rape, and pestilence. Crops will fail and children will be kidnapped. The

---

1. Erlander, *Manna and Mercy*, 6.

people will experience defeat, starvation, thirst, and cannibalism, and will be scattered around the Earth.

- In Num 31, God orders vengeance. Israelites are instructed to massacre every Midianite they encounter—except females who are virgins. Such women and girls the Israelite men are instructed to kidnap, compel into marriage, and rape. Really?

- In Deut 7 and 20 and throughout the books of Joshua and Judges, as the Israelites make their way into the so-called promised land, God commands them to "clear away" and "utterly destroy" the residents of the lands they pass through. They are to "show no mercy" (Deut 7:1–2 NRSV); "take as your booty the women, the children, livestock, and everything else in the town" (Deut 20:14 NRSV); and sometimes even kill "everything that breathes" (Deut 20:16 NRSV). In Josh 10:26, along with exterminating Canaanite inhabitants, God orders Joshua to hang and impale the five Amorite kings of Jerusalem, Hebron, Jarmuth, Lachish, and Eglon. Much in the books of Joshua and Judges involves stories of God-ordered crimes, including theft of land, slavery, and killing rampages.[2]

- In 1 Sam 15:1–9, the newly crowned King Saul is commanded by God to commit homicide and biocide, to kill Amalekite men, women, children, infants, oxen, sheep, camels, and donkeys "with the edge of the sword" (1 Sam 15:8 NRSV).

- When the Judahites engage in false worship in Jer 7 and 19, God sets the Babylonians upon them to slaughter the Judahites in the streets, leaving their corpses for birds to devour. Survivors resort to cannibalizing their children and neighbors.

- Ps 137:9 and several other psalms portray the Deity as ordering Israelites to slay their enemies, including dashing Babylonian children against the rocks (similar to what Nazi troopers did to Jewish children and babies).

2. Approximately 90 percent of today's video games played by children, youth, and adults include violence or glorify violence. Popular games such as *Mortal Kombat* and *Grand Theft Auto* give participants virtual experiences in killing. These killings are always portrayed as righteous and heroic. What is the numbing effect?

- The book of Job is a parable. In chapters 1–2 especially, God tests Job's faith by murdering Job and his wife's offspring, destroying their livestock, and inflicting afflictions on Job's body.

What should we make of these stories? They are not the whole biblical story, certainly. But they are in the Bible. Could it be that the writers of these stories underachieved, especially in their attempt to present the heart of God? Might it be that civil religion (God and country) and even military propaganda mistakenly got inserted into parts of the Bible? In the New Testament also, but much less so, when Ananias and Sapphira hold back from sharing their wealth with others, the writer implies that God strikes them dead (Acts 5:1–11).

Even today, some theologies insist on portraying God as a justifiably wrathful, bad-guy Father, with Jesus being the grace-filled, good-guy Son who mediates for us by appeasing his dad through crucifixion.[3] A truer interpretation, in my view, is that Jesus shows us what God truly is like, at times more faithfully than does the Bible.

ॐ

Reflection Questions

1. Though "hidden in plain sight," the troubling stories I mention are usually overlooked by interpreters and even softened by translators. What impact do these stories have on your theology?

2. Does propaganda, military or otherwise, sometimes make it into the Bible? What should we do with such troubling stories? What surprises you about your answer?

---

3. Several atonement theories are based on this scenario. I will be critiquing these theories in chapter 14.

Chapter 12

God's Secondary Mission: Israel
(Continued)

As God's secondary mission of trying to heal a wayward species continues, God next establishes a *chosen people*. Where might the Divinity search for a chosen people? In the halls of power? Among the upper classes? Middle classes? In institutions of higher learning? From the echelons of social or religious privilege? Among the rank and file? It is notable that when God travels to Egypt in search of a chosen people, God's heart is drawn to folks at the bottom. God selects a people whose labor, livelihood, and very lives are being stolen by others, people who subsist under the steel boot of oppression. In the ensuing Exodus account, God dramatically rescues a group of Hebrew slaves from Egypt and thrusts them into the Sinai Desert for forty years of what Daniel Erlander calls "wilderness school."[1]

Pharaoh's Egypt is typical of Cain-ism's values, worldviews, and behaviors. The diagram below is an adaptation of a helpful diagram created by Daniel Erlander.[2]

1. Erlander, *Manna and Mercy*, 48.
2. Erlander, *Manna and Mercy*, 4.

Pharaoh's Egypt

Cain's world

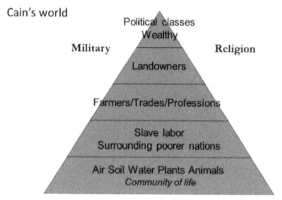

adapted from Daniel Erlander

In this diagram of Cain's world, the top levels of the pyramid are reserved for those with access to power, wealth, land, and military backing. These people and their institutions are in command of the system and benefit most from it. The setup serves them very well. Beneath these top echelons, in increasing population percentages, are the everyday workers, such as farmers, plus those working in various trades and professions. These folks live more on the edge. Next come slaves and those who work for slave wages, followed by the people and markets of surrounding and distant poorer nations. All these serve as prey in Cain-ism's horde of hoarders. Finally, bearing the weight and brunt of the pyramid setup are the multilayered ecosystems and species diversities of God's beloved household, the diverse and threatened community of life. Cain prides himself in his ability to have his boot on Nature's throat.

Notice in the diagram that "military power" is closely linked with the setup of Cain and Pharaoh. Through violence, the threat of violence, and the appearance of the threat of violence, the military is used to covertly and overtly *leverage* the world in Cain's favor, especially politically and economically. The system's defenses ensure the necessary teeth for Cain's exploitive deeds.

But along with military power, significantly and sadly, the other keeper and protector of Cain-ism's setup is religion. Religion sanctifies the arrangement. Religion bestows sacred cover. It allows Cain to claim that his way of life is ordained by God.[3]

What should we make of this? It is important to realize that God does not set the Israelites free in order for them to be free. Freedom can be a false god like anything else. Numerous nations, including the United States, have committed genocide, ecocide, biocide, and other anti-God atrocities in the name of freedom and liberty. Rather, the LORD sets the Israelites free in order to teach them a better way of living.[4]

Also, it should be noted that God does not set the Israelites free so they can now move up the ladder. God's goal is not to preserve the pyramid system with the caveat that next time, the Israelites will reside on top and others below. Rather, the LORD sets the Israelites free and sends them to "wilderness school" so that God can teach them a more excellent Abel way, an alternative to the very smart but unintelligent, non-wise, and unethical ways of Pharaoh's Egypt and Cain's world. God even hopes that after a time of careful instruction, these chosen folks will become wise and ethical teachers to the rest of their species, as portrayed in the book of Isaiah:

3. The French tyrant Napoleon Bonaparte (1769–1821) understood well the utilitarian benefits of religion, saying, "As for me, I do not see in religion the mystery of the Incarnation, only the mystery of the Social Order. How can one have order in a State without religion? Society cannot exist without inequality of wealth and inequality of wealth cannot exist without religion. When a man is dying of hunger next to another who is gorging, he cannot possibly accept this difference if he has not had it on good authority that God wishes it so; there must be poor and rich in the world, but afterwards, for eternity, things will be divided up differently" (Zamoyski, *Napoleon: A Life*, 299).

4. We recall that American slave traders and slaveholders deemed legal restrictions on their operations as attacks on liberty. In our time, companies that pollute God's creation also often see antipollution legislation as infringing on their freedoms. Freedom and liberty can be perverse idols, especially when used to excuse violence, greed, and ecological irresponsibility.

In the days to come the mountain of the LORD's house shall be established as the highest of mountains, and shall be raised above the hills; all nations shall stream to it. Many peoples shall say, 'Come, let us go up to the mountain of the LORD, to the house of the God of Jacob; that he may teach us his ways and that we may walk in his paths.' For out of Zion shall go forth instruction, and the word of the LORD from Jerusalem. He shall judge between the nations and shall arbitrate for many peoples. They shall beat their swords into plowshares and their spears into pruning hooks. Nation shall not lift up sword against nation; neither shall they learn war any more. (Isa 2:2–4 NRSV; also Mic 4:1–4)

But alas, too many Israelites equate "chosen-ness" with privilege. They think their calling is to status rather than service. Soon Israel's leaders are behaving just like Pharaoh, and Israel's citizens just like the Egyptian public. Regrettably, such assumed privilege distorts the faith of many Christians too.

Along with the chosen-people experiment, God also institutes a system of *laws*. Laws are necessary; laws are good. Every society needs wise regulations to assist in bringing order and fairness as individuals, communities, and nations journey through the ups and downs and give and take of human interaction. But alas, laws do not heal. They don't transform our inner spirits, souls, and selves. Laws can even be used to advance injustice, a reality to which history all too often attests.[5]

---

5. I have written already about US laws regarding race. A White legal system enshrined slavery for generations. In a war of rebellion (1861–65), White Americans killed to defend this racism. After losing the war, they wrote and enforced laws that allowed them to snatch victory out of defeat and to institutionalize White rule. Not just in the South but around the nation, today's conservatives (the Confederacy's twenty-first-century personification) are dedicated to preserving this advantage.

Laws have also sanctioned dubious acts of war making, including the Bush-Cheney-Rumsfeld "designer war" in 2003 against the people of Iraq. Cain leaders can always find a pretext to justify any war. Under the guise of false patriotism, it is often easy to dupe and rally support.

Also, laws continue to be ghostwritten by lobbyists whose companies can then get away with polluting God's creation.

ᄋᆈ

God also invites the Israelites into the land of Canaan—the so-called *promised land*—to live peacefully and respectfully among the current inhabitants, who with their homes, businesses, farms, and fields have been dwelling in these properties for millennia. But alas, the Israelites mistake God's invitation and their new neighbor's cautious hospitality to mean "manifest destiny." So armed, they become conquistadors. The Israelites end up committing land thievery, demolishment of homes and villages, enslavement of others, genocide, ecocide, and biocide. The biblical books of Joshua and Judges chronicle as heroic these troubling deeds and occurrences. The writers even try to make it seem as though God is ordering the terrorism. In my view, as stated earlier, such disinformation sometimes mistakenly got included in the Hebrew Scriptures.

"Manifest destiny" happened in North and South America too, as White agents of Cain-ism from Europe and the United States engaged in State-sponsored terror. As mentioned before, the foundation for this misbehavior is known as the "Doctrine of Discovery." This was enshrined by way of landmark legislation and rulings by the United States Supreme Court through numerous government policy decisions, including the Monroe Doctrine, and ultimately in the manifesto called "Manifest Destiny" (a term coined in 1845 by New York newspaper editor John O'Sullivan).[6] The result was the near extinction on this continent of countless Native peoples.

Along with this, Manifest Destiny also justified ecocide and biocide. By the middle of the 1860s, approximately four hundred million North American beavers had been slaughtered on this continent, and by the end of the 1800s, nearly seventy million Great Plains buffalo were exterminated. The beavers were slain solely for the furs sold to wealthy buyers in Europe, China, Russia, and the US East Coast. Buffalos were executed in concert with White America's land theft and genocide against Native families. This slaughter destroyed a major food, clothing, and shelter resource for Native

---

6. McPherson, *The War That Forged a Nation*, 16.

families, working in tandem with other US policies of relocation, reeducation, forced treaties, broken treaties, and extermination.[7]

All this demonstrates again the sobering truth—namely, that Cain-ism's explosive narrative will always lead to Abel's oppression and a conquistador modus operandi toward God's creation. There is no such thing as a "nicer" version of Cain.

ᐁ

The Hebrew Scriptures also describe the reigns of Israel's *kings*. It is important to remember that God despises Israel's request for a king (1 Sam 8). Why? Because Israel already has a king—the LORD. However, the Israelites are filled with envy as they eye the military power, international status, and material appliances of their neighbors who have kings. They keep begging and pleading. Eventually God yields, but not without this foresight warning sent through the prophet Samuel:

> Samuel reported all the words of the LORD to the people who were asking him for a king. He said, 'These will be the ways of the king who will reign over you; he will take your sons and appoint them to his chariots and to be his horsemen, and to run before his chariots; and he will appoint for himself commanders of thousands and commanders of fifties, and some to plow his ground and to reap his harvest, and to make his implements of war and the equipment of his chariots.
>
> He will take your daughters to be perfumers and cooks and bakers. He will take the best of your fields and vineyards and olive orchards and give them to his courtiers. He will take one-tenth of your grain and of your vineyards and give it to his officers and his courtiers. He will take your male and female slaves, and the best of your cattle and donkeys, and put them to his work. He will take one-tenth of your flocks, and you shall be his slaves. And

7. Think of the unconscionable waste. Herds of buffalo, if managed and harvested with intelligence and wisdom and ethics, would have provided a never-ending blessing to the soil and an almost unlimited nutritional food source for other animals and humans for generation upon generation. Instead, the herds were cruelly, foolishly, and wastefully decimated.

in that day, you will cry out because of your king, whom you have chosen for yourselves; but the Lord will not answer you in that day." (1 Sam 8:10–18 NRSV)

Israel does not listen. Although Israelite kings like Saul (1020–1000 BCE, see 1 Sam 13–31), David (1000–961 BCE, see 2 Sam 9–20; 1 Kgs 1–2), and Solomon (961–922 BCE, see 1 Kgs 1–11) each begin their tenures somewhat honorably, they soon become rotten to the core. As forecasted by the Lord and by Samuel, the kings of Israel and their courts become more interested in acquiring and keeping power for themselves and their nation than in serving God, God's creation, and humanity.

By the way, neither King David's rape of Bathsheba nor his murder of Bathsheba's husband Uriah the Hittite (2 Sam 11:2–27) should be seen solely as an episode of personal failure. It is this, certainly. However, it is also a metaphor for bigger crimes. Such behavior on the part of this Cain king is how all Abel cultures, ecosystems, and species experience directly and indirectly the malfeasance of Cain-ism's violent narrative.[8]

And even though King Solomon starts off nobly (1 Kgs 3:7–10), he too soon regresses into Cain-ism. Because he can, he hoards. He becomes addicted to concupiscence (gathering all things unto oneself). He behaves in conquistador fashion toward Israel's neighbors. He accumulates seven hundred wives and three hundred girlfriends for his personal harem: "King Solomon loved many foreign women along with the daughter of Pharaoh . . . Among Solomon's wives were seven hundred princesses and three hundred concubines" (1 Kgs 11:1, 3 NRSV). And he oversees the construction of a religious temple in Jerusalem, supposedly in honor of the Lord, by the sweat, injuries, and deaths of cadres of slaves. Could anything be more contrary to what God expects of humans, especially from those who claim to be God's special people?

8. The use of the word "rape" may seem controversial. However, surely when a married woman is summoned by an all-powerful king to visit him, and within minutes his penis is ejaculating into her vagina, this hardly seems like committed and loving sexual intimacy. Likewise, the designation of "murderer" for King David also is appropriate in that he organizes Uriah's death. This is to cover up the fact that King David impregnates Bathsheba.

After the relatively brief United Monarchy period (1020-922 BCE), the region split into the Northern Kingdom and Southern Kingdom. Subsequent Hebrew kings of these regions continued to engage in Cain-ism's unintelligent, non-wise, and non-ethical behaviors. The kings of the North include Jeroboam I, Omri, Ahab, Jehu, Jeroboam II, and Pekah. This region collapses in 721 BCE. at the hands of a neighboring Cain (Assyria). The kings of the South include Jehoshaphat, Jehoram, Ahaziah, Jehoash, Uzziah, Jotham, Ahaz, Hezekiah, Manasseh, Josiah, Jehoiakim, Jehoiachin, Zedekiah, and queen Athaliah (842–837 BCE). This region collapses in 587 BCE at the hands of another Cain neighbor (Babylon), and many residents become exiles in Babylon.[9]

Lastly, throughout Old Testament times God sends *prophets* and *people of wisdom* who dedicate their lives to speaking truth. Among these servants of God are people like Elijah, Joel, Huldah, Amos, Micah, Jeremiah, Deborah, Malachi, Isaiah, and the many people whose writings are collected in the book of Proverbs. These inspired and courageous people do their best to cut through the "socially constructed moral oblivion" that undergirds Cain-ism's systems.[10]

In her book *Resisting Structural Evil: Love as Ecological-Economic Vocation,* Dr. Cynthia Moe-Lobeda explores the main ingredients utilized by Cain-ism to maintain "socially constructed moral oblivion." A numb populace is essential in Cain's world. The eight ingredients for maintaining this numbness are as follows: 1) "Privatized Morality and the Blinders of Charity"; 2) "Blessings Veiling Stolen Goods"; 3) "Denial, Guilt, Grief"; 4) "Despair or Hopelessness and Perceived Powerlessness"; 5) "Unconscious Conformity";

9. As a side note, the language of "king" and "kingdom" when talking about God is always problematic. I can think of few human models in history where this kind of political/economic/social set-up even comes close to reflecting Godly values, worldviews, or behaviors. Such constructs are more in line with the pyramid systems of Pharaoh's Egypt and Cain's world. Even in the Lord's Prayer, I prefer to substitute "kin-dom" for "kingdom," as in: "Thy kin-dom come, thy will be done." This seems much closer to what Jesus had in mind in my view.

10. Moe-Lobeda, *Resisting Structural Evil*, 90.

6) "Corporate Investment in Maintaining Public Moral Oblivion";
7) "Uncritical Belief in 'Growth' as Good"; and 8) "Moral Oblivion
Embedded in Practice."[11] The entire book is meticulously researched,
and this section is especially insightful. Moe-Lobeda is a prophetic
woman of wisdom who like saints of old gives full voice to both the
pastoral word of God and the prophetic word of God. Her book challenges Cain's foul justifications for rifling through Abel's world with
indifference. It convicts Cain-ism's politics, economics, ecological
misbehaviors, justice systems, and faith.

The Old Testament is filled with stories of God's intention to heal
and restore Israel and *Homo sapiens*, but writers and leaders and
citizens often fail to get it right. Law, chosen people, promised
land—the people fail to understand why they were set free from
Pharoah's system. Kings, wise women and wise men, prophets—
they ignore God's efforts at healing and restoration. As these attempts are dissembled by Cain-ism, they fall short in effecting the
desired aim. We are left wondering: Is there anything left? What can
be done? What will the Creator do?

Reflection Questions

1. Discuss the diagram of Pharaoh's Egypt/Cain's world. Are
   there similarities today?
2. Why are laws necessary? Why do they not have the power to
   heal people?
3. How have both the Doctrine of Discovery and Manifest Destiny worked against God's mission? Did you have teachers
   growing up who framed these ideologies as positive? Or as
   neutral sidebar issues?
4. Discuss Cynthia Moe-Lobeda's insights regarding "socially
   constructed moral oblivion."

11. Moe-Lobeda, *Resisting Structural Evil*, 90–106.

Chapter 13

God's Secondary Mission: Jesus

FINALLY, AT LONG LAST, God the Creator and Mother and Father and lover and forgiver and renewer and challenger and ground of all being decides to come *in person*. This is the Christian story/message/claim. Humanity's problem is that Cain's penchant for dominion-ism has become *the* dominant and domineering narrative of our species. It is the air we breathe and the airwaves that inculcate us 24/7. Most of us, myself included, mindlessly act out Cain-ism's narrative without giving it a thought in our private, public, national, business, and household lives—and for Christians, even in our church lives. As Cain-plagued people, we have become so numbed and accustomed to living out of relationship with neighbor, Nature, our own inner soul/spirit/self, and God that we think this is normal. We think this is the only way to live and move and have our being.

The Danish philosopher, theologian, and poet Soren Kierkegaard (1813–55), called this regressed state of disconnectedness a "sickness unto death."[1] German theologian Paul Tillich (1886–1965) uses the term "dis-ease."[2] For Saint Paul in Rom 8:22 (RSV), it is a "groaning in travail" affecting arenas beyond the merely human. A friend of mine uses the phrase "existential disrepair."

---

1. See Kierkegaard, *Sickness unto Death*.

2. See Tillich, "The Meaning of Health." Tillich did not include the hyphen; my seminary professor always used the hyphen for emphasis when writing on the blackboard.

Another word might be "perishing."

Consider this: Did Jesus come with the intention of overcoming death? In my view the answer is no. Death is a part of life, just as God intended it. It is *tov*. It is not just life's joys and sorrows that "come to pass," but living itself actually passes too. Everything that has ever lived and breathed has also died. As a Christian, I believe in the resurrection of the dead and I believe in heaven. Though admittedly covered in great mystery, this is a breathtaking hope. This hope not only gives me courage and peace of mind to face the ups and downs of daily life, but it also helps me face my own mortality and that of my loved ones.

The gifts of resurrection and heaven, however, come *after* death. This new birth comes after living for a while, and then dying. We cannot bypass death. And because of this, life is to be cherished, but never hoarded.

The mission of Jesus does not bypass death, for himself or for us. What his mission does do is zero in on the disorder of perishing. What is perishing? To be perishing is to be out of relationship—with my human neighbor, with Nature, with my own inner spirit/soul/self, and with God. This is what Jesus came to heal.

In addition to the Creator seeking to address Cain's lost condition by means of a flood parable, fashioning a chosen people, and inviting ex-enslaved refugees into respectful residency in an already occupied land, and by way of laws, kings, and prophets, God also sent many other Abel figures over the centuries. These personages have appeared in the form of rabbis, sages, indigenous folks, people on the margins, outcasts, and most significantly, the prophetic wisdom of God's "still, small voice" in Nature (1 Kgs 19:12 RSV). God is determined to heal our wayward species—thanks be to God.

So finally, God decided to come in person. This is the heart of the Christian gospel.

However, God cannot actually appear in person. Why? Because God is too big, too awesome. The Deity is unimaginably uncontainable, and infinitely overwhelming. We would all have heart attacks in God's actual presence—acute myocardial infarctions. Therefore, in the poetic and liturgical language of Saint Paul in his letter to the Philippians (2:5–11), the eternal Christ of God *empties* self of self and very God of very God and enters humanity. The Christ of God shows up in a microbe-colonized, warm-blooded, hairy, placental, backboned, and mortal mammal of the species *Homo sapiens*—Jesus of Nazareth. This is quite a miracle, to which Christian theology has attached the term "incarnation."

Have you ever wondered why God chose to show up in human form and not as something else? The eternal Christ of God is not a human figure, just like the eternal Christ of God is not a horse or a bristlecone pine tree or a desert beetle. I suppose if horses had been the species gone amiss and awry, a horse would have been born in Bethlehem. Or if pine trees and desert beetles had not been living honorably, these would have been the creatures needing lodging on that holy night. But it was the human creature who was at war with God and with what God holds dear. It was the human creature who was lost, and Jesus came "to seek and to save the lost" (Luke 19:10 RSV).

What would Christ's message be? What transformational narrative would Jesus embody and proclaim? For me, the message is simply and profoundly this: "*Homo sapiens*, you are forgiven; follow me."

"You are forgiven." What does this part mean? It means: "*Homo sapiens*, you are forgiven for being at war with your neighbor, with my creation, with your own inner soul/spirit/self, and with me. I am going to forgive you for this warfare today, tomorrow, and every day in the future. You are pardoned. Pure gift. Pure grace. Pure love. You are forgiven." Jesus lived this blessing and practiced it in his healings, teachings, exorcisms, conflicts with the powers and principalities, temptations, rejections by friends, and refusal to take up violence as a way to solve problems. He also lived and practiced the blessing by the manner in which he "beheld" the lilies of the field and the birds of the air, in his cross life, in his cross death, and in his new-birth resurrection. Jesus wants us to be overtaken by this blessing of grace. He wants this holy gift to protect, enwrap, strengthen, and enthrall us at all times and in all places, through every up and down, Gloria and Kyrie, and blessing and bummer on life's journey. Forgiveness is God's initial, daily repeated, and ongoing loving *embrace*.

However, forgiveness is not the Christian gospel. It isn't even a new thing that Jesus brings. God was doing this long before Bethlehem, Galilee, and Jerusalem. Also, forgiveness alone is not God's ultimate goal. God doesn't say: "I forgive you human beings—everything is okay now. I am fine; we are fine. Now go write a bunch of praise songs and liturgies telling me how wonderful you think I am to forgive you for messing up my world." No, the Deity's ultimate goal is not forgiveness for our species. Rather, it is the healing of our species.

So, accompanying God's forgiveness are two of the most important words in the Bible—namely, "Follow me." This phrase appears dozens of times in the New Testament. And not just follow *me* as opposed to following someone or something else, but *follow* me as opposed to staying where you are. "*Follow* me. Come along with me. I will walk with you. You walk with me. We will go together. Staying where you are is not an option. We are going places."

"But follow you where, Jesus?" we ask.

- "Follow me; I want you to meet your *neighbor*." Of course, Jesus reminds me that "neighbor" does not just refer to people I like or people like me. Rather, my neighbor is every person, especially the stranger (and "strange" one), outcast, alien (and "illegal" alien), widow and widower, orphan, and person who lives in want and poverty. It is even my enemy (Matt 5:43, 48). Neighbor is the "other."

The subject of immigration puts current flesh on this invitation/calling/command. Immigration is a complicated issue and I have no recommendation as to what policies are best. There are many factors involved, and ethical and knowledgeable leaders of goodwill need to be implementing honorable policies with due diligence and in good faith. Unfortunately, this is not happening.

However, while I do not know what the ultimate answer is, I do know that characterizations of our asylum-seeking neighbors as anything other than beloved by Jesus Christ and worthy of everyone's utmost respect are on the side of evil. Such calumnies are in the anti-God camp. No policy of credible justice will ever come from such I-centered ideologies.[3]

So, Jesus the risen Christ today says: "Follow me; I want you to meet your neighbor. I want to bring you face to face and heart to heart into the crucibles of life. Why? Because this is where my kind of healing takes place." Maybe you give haircuts to homeless men at a local soup kitchen, or volunteer at the hospital to hold and cuddle babies with spina bifida or opioid addiction or who will die soon, and your job is to simply hold them and love them.[4] Perhaps you assist a neighbor in shopping for groceries because she is losing her world to dementia, or you carry water to migrants crossing dangerous desert borders to save their lives. Abel of Nazareth, the risen and living Christ, calls each of us today in different and dramatic ways out of our realms of relative ease into "harm's way." Why? Jesus wants us to meet his and our neighbor in a way that will change us, so that people in need will be helped and *we* will never be the same.[5]

3. Only villains rip children from their families. Jesus does not condone any kind of I-centeredness, including "America First." A person seeking asylum is not an "illegal" in any honorable country. Families in situations of desperation find it nearly impossible to navigate the dysfunctional US immigration system. This dysfunction is not their fault. It is the fault of US voters and their elected officials. Also, while cross-border drug trafficking is a significant problem, one also must wonder why Americans are such a high-potential market. What personal and national emptiness is feeding this elevated demand?

4. I had the opportunity to do this with my campus-ministry students in a very poor area of Haiti at Mother Theresa's Baby Hospital. There were a variety of circumstances in this loving place. Some infants and toddlers had families; others did not. A few would get well; many would not. Several children lay listless in our arms, while others clung desperately to us in fear. Did we help these children? A little. Did the experience change my students and me? Yes, profoundly.

5. A story is told about Mother Theresa (1910–97). A respected journalist travels across the globe to interview this legendary Christian woman. A few minutes into the conversation Mother Theresa announces dryly, "I'm not very interesting." Then, pointing, she quietly invites, "Why don't you talk with that boy in the corner? He'll probably die tonight." Her scheme is not to get out of the interview, or even to have the journalist interview the boy. Her aim is

- Jesus also says: "Follow me; I want you to meet my *creation*, the multilayered ecosystems and species diversities of Nature. *Homo sapiens*, you are behaving badly. You daily disregard what I cherish. You assert your desires above mine and trash my beloved in frightful ways. Sacred and carefully embedded patterns are being distorted by your behavior. Cain and all admirers of Cain-ism, you are in need of profound reconstruction. I forgive you today and will continue to forgive you tomorrow, but you need to come with me back into the Mother/Father/Creator's household. You need to learn again how to live honorably amidst the dwelling places with and within all my family. Follow me to meet God's household, God's creation."

There are people in the US today, mostly mainstream conservatives, who are choosing to be insensible. They are intentionally denying or ignoring the wealth of evidence coming from dozens of scientific fields regarding human-caused ecological degradation. These leaders and their underlings in government, industry, and the media are doing everything they can to thwart ecologically responsible policies and behaviors. This is negligence. This is intelligence and wisdom gone missing. Such ideologies are on the side of harm. Many of these folks seem to be proud of their anti-science, pro-pollution, anti-God, and bellicose Cain-strutting agenda. In my opinion, they should be disenfranchised from voting and from leadership until they can find release from their deadening ideology.[6]

---

more conspiratorial. She wants this visitor to sit with the boy, and maybe even hold him through the night while he dies of poverty. She wants the journalist's senses, heart, and spirit. She wants to "save" this traveler and help him reconnect with the community of life. Who knows, this journalist might even ask himself, "Why is this boy dying? What is his name? What has been his story? Why do I feel so helpless? What needs healing in me and the systems and structures that favor me to the detriment of others?" The journalist's life might even find restoration, all because he meets his neighbor.

6. Two conversation stoppers are often invoked when businesses or industries get caught being ecologically irresponsible. The first is "It creates jobs." According to such thinking, almost any enterprise that produces a job is considered justified. But are not some jobs dishonorable? Isn't a business that pollutes God's creation outside the perimeters of integrity? Can these workers be

Some of the college students I served as a campus pastor would at times have minor and major problems with roommates and housemates. They were learning that living with others is quite challenging and that housemates can be considerate, or they can be inconsiderate. Some wash their dishes immediately after eating; others leave them dirty for days. One person may keep the noise level low while another is clueless that they are bothering others. Wastefulness regarding utilities often caused conflict. What grade do you think most humans deserve vis-à-vis the other twenty million species in God's household? Are we behaving as responsible housemates? Cain is offended by this question. The house belongs to us, after all (in Cain's imagination). In contrast, Abel and Jesus know the weight of this question.

The good news is that approximately 85 percent of the most dangerous human-caused ecological damage is being committed by about 15 percent of Earth's human population. This is good news because it means the whole human species doesn't need conversion. What is even better news is that, of the 15 percent doing 85 percent of the damage, Americans make up nearly one-half of these. As difficult as it may be to change ourselves, it would be infinitely more daunting if we had to revise the entire human family (over 7.9 billion people currently). The best news of all, however, is this: of the 15 percent doing 85 percent of the damage, nearly one-half of whom are Americans, approximately one-half of these see themselves as Christians. What if Christians in the 15 percent could be converted to following Jesus? Don't we know that "The Earth is the LORD's, and the fulness thereof" (Ps 24:1 RSV)? Aren't we trying to follow Jesus because he is the "way, truth, and life" (John 14:6 RSV)? Christians work in and make decisions in every commercial, governmental, educational, nonprofit, and household industry on the planet. What would happen if a majority of Christians became

---

proud of what they do? Should consumers purchase such goods and services?

The other behavior-justifying conversation stopper is this: "There are trade-offs. Some bad must be done for the greater good." The problem is that "trade-off" thinking is triumphing. It is winning the day to unwieldly and damaging effect. It has taken on a life of its own. The mega-trends of these accrued trade-offs are systematically degrading God's household.

faithful? Might this have a positive effect on the biosphere, including on our species? Could the body of Christ become a model teacher, and become part of the world's "thin thread of hope," and even perhaps be a living force for good?

I do have hope that many of the 15 percent can be converted to following the risen Christ, including me as an American and Christian. However, in the meantime, I am also mindful of what the besieged 85 percent in their more despairing moments might be inclined to do with their justifiable rage toward us. They suffer disproportionately from the ecological damage we bring to Earth's ecosystems. As climate volatility, declining biodiversity, rising sea levels, droughts, floods, increased insect infestations, species extinctions, new disease outbreaks, and other degradations attack their homelands, will they be able to disarm Cain-ism's terror in time? Also, will Cain find wisdom and be able to respond with repentance, amendment of life, and restitution? Or will Cain-ism's most prominent countries choose to respond with guns and missiles, easily lying to themselves and others? Will the ultimate loyalty of Christians in the 15 percent be to God, or to country? Such a dilemma should not be difficult for true followers of Jesus Christ. However, the fact that it is reveals the extent and success of Cain-ism's numbing indoctrinations.

- Jesus says: "Follow me; you even need to meet your own *inner soul/spirit/self.* The disconnectedness living within your soul is eating you up and generating spiritual emptiness. You roam the Earth searching for titillations. You end up filling your dispirited void with nonsense. Follow me, beloved. You need to meet yourself. You need to learn to respect this person I have created, whom I love no more and no less than all the other creatures in my household."

- Finally, Jesus says: "Follow me; I want you to meet your Father, Mother, *Creator*—the true one above all others, who holds everything, including this Earth, including your neighbor, including all of Nature, and including you." This dangerous but healing encounter takes place in the realms of worship, prayer, baptism, Lord's Supper, meditation, spiritual direction, and more.

Jesus wants us to know the Creator through him, whether we are experiencing feelings of closeness or feelings of distance. He wants us to be daily shaped by the joy and assurance of a wild and healing relationship of promise with God. He wants our truculent narrative and disruptive behavior to be mended and amended.

Embedded in these arenas of life are the following words from the Hebrew psalmist, resonating with what our often-disjointed souls long for most deeply:

> "Create in me a clean heart, O God,
>   and renew a right spirit within me.
> Cast me not away from your presence,
>   and take not your holy spirit from me.
> Restore unto me the joy of your salvation,
>   and uphold me with your free spirit."
> (A common version of Psalm 51:10-12 used in Lutheran worship)

I fully embrace the bold Christian proclamation that Jesus the risen Christ is alive today. The secondary mission of God is alive and well and walking the Earth in the twenty-first century calling and coaxing each human into vigilance, saying: "Daughter, son, child, sibling, you are forgiven; follow me. My grace and forgiveness are sufficient to empower your soul. Follow me today and tomorrow. Where? Follow me into the Creator's household, wherein dwell neighbor, creation, your own inner soul/spirit/self, and me." This household of God is not languishing back in Bible times or back anywhere in the past. It is here today, in between our toes and in front of our faces. As Saint Paul joyfully declares, "The word is near you, on your lips and in your heart" (Rom 10:8 NRSV). Also: "Now is the acceptable time; see, now is the day of salvation" (2 Cor 6:2b NRSV).

Christians are people who know this. Christians are people who cling to the risen Christ's forgiveness and who courageously go with him into transformative places of relational healing. Congregations of Christians joyfully bask in unending forgiveness and have as their holy agenda to follow Jesus into situations of healing with (1) neighbor, (2) Creation, (3) their inner souls, and (4) God. (These may be the only four committees essential to a congregation's calling and task.)

Who is this eternal Christ of God, this incarnate Abel of Nazareth? In his letter to the Ephesians, Saint Paul describes the risen Christ this way:

> He is our peace . . . breaking down the dividing wall of hostility . . . that he might create in himself a new humanity . . . He came and proclaimed peace to those far off and those near . . . So then, you are no longer strangers and aliens . . . but citizens of the household of God. (Eph 2:14–19 NRSV)

Reflection Questions

1. Does it make sense to you that Jesus came not to overcome death, but to overcome perishing?
2. Do you wonder why the eternal Christ of God showed up in human form? Does my explanation make sense to you?
3. "You are forgiven; follow me." Does this declaration and command get at the heart of the Christian gospel for you?
4. When and where have you recently gone with the risen Christ into "harm's way" and found restoration of relationship with neighbor, Nature, self, or God?

Chapter 14

Reassessing Original Sin and the Atonement Theories

"ABEL CHRISTIANITY" MIGHT BE an appropriate name for the version of the Christian faith I am presenting. This version/narrative/worldview/gospel is at odds with Cain-ism. Abel Christianity takes another look at God's story of life, especially in light of new learnings from Nature's natural sciences. It also understands the human predicament as a fall into I-centeredness as individuals, as nations, and as a species. It obliges an invigorated reframing and refreshed recasting of God's response in the story of Israel and the story of Jesus.

Forthwith, in my opinion, at least two weighty Christian teachings require re-examination. These are the doctrine of original sin and the major theories of the atonement.

Original sin: Cain's ignoble embrace of I-centeredness is recent, not original. Although three hundred thousand years of Abel living should never be romanticized—Abel is *tov*, not perfect or even close to it—unlike Cain, Abel has not lived as though our species is separate from, superior to, the reason for, or the ruler of God's Earth. Thus, Abel cultures have generally lived viscerally and philosophically and even theologically with and within the sphere of God's intentions and Earth's wise checks and balances. Such mature living has enabled humans to creatively adapt and evolve for tens of thousands of years.

Cain's break from Abel living, on the other hand, is recent. This wily attempt to live exempt from Nature and over and against Nature only began gaining traction during the past six thousand to ten thousand years. Today's humans in most cultures are products of Cain's version of life. We are "marinated in our mother's womb" in the placental fluids of Cain-ism's narrative. It is the only thing we know. However—and this is indeed good news—this narrative is not representative of the totality of our species' longer-held character, nor is it inevitable. The ascendance of this perfidy to the status of dominance is a recent aberration.[1]

The doctrine of original sin implies that because Adam and Eve (either as actual first parents or as timeless representatives of the entirety of human history) were disobedient, all humans are sin-*full* and fated to go the way of Taker-ism. This easily becomes an alibi for reckless behavior. If we are destroying God's household on Earth, what is the big surprise? There is original sin, after all. If we glorify war and bestow legitimacy on weapons of mass destruction, why would we expect otherwise? If racism abounds, this is just our human nature. Humanity is shackled; humanity is fallen.

The doctrine even entangles Earth's ecosystems and species diversities into the kingdoms of Cain-ism. Nature is a beast, it says. This is a fallen dog-eat-dog world. We do well to attack Nature before it attacks us. Human sin brought this fallen condition about. Now there are hurricanes, earthquakes, diseases, thistles, illness, and mosquitoes. Now there is even dying and death.

This, of course, is silly. Such events are not the result of human sin any more than is a brown bear tracking down and eating a White-tailed deer for her dinner (or a human catching and eating a

---

1. Again, Abel is not to be romanticized or demonized. Abel is neither saint nor fiend. Along with activities such as farming, hunting, finding spouses, raising kids, getting a cold or the flu, moving to new locations, building, thinking, feeling, and dying, Abel also at times fights over territory, overfishes waters, and in the past even possibly contributed to the extinction of the saber-toothed tiger, mammoth, and mastodon. But the degree is minuscule (a mole hill) compared to Cain-ism's mountain of misdeeds. The checks and balances of Earth can handle Abel's impact. Abel is only seeking a livelihood among life's contenders. Cain, on the other hand, seeks dominance. Cain even normalizes the annihilation of other housemates in God's household.

trout). These are natural *tov* processes in God's world. *Tov* isn't outside of God's intentions. It is not even deficient or inferior to heaven. It is *tov*. Heaven will be *tov*, too, though probably in different ways. And certainly, the sin of Adam and Eve did not trigger a need for the whole cosmos to be redeemed. No, God's universe is fine. It is *tov*.[2]

ᔕ

Atonement: There are also several theories of the atonement that require reconsideration. Christian theologians and ecumenical church councils have worked hard throughout the centuries to explain Jesus' crucifixion on the cross, a horrific deed of capital punishment carried out in the name of Cain's religious and political values. These atonement theories are attempts to answer questions such as "Why did Jesus die?" and "Why in that brutal manner?" Below is a brief explanation of four common atonement theories:

- *Sacrificial theory of the atonement:* This theory argues that the sacrificial system as presented in the Hebrew Bible is God-ordained. God set it up. God was not only pleased that Abraham was willing to sacrifice his and Sarah's son Isaac to God (Gen 22), but also that Israel strove to carry out animal and grain sacrifices in Jerusalem as a way of atoning for their sins. In this view, the sacrificial system was God's idea.

If you apply this scenario to the Jesus story, then, Jesus easily gets presented as another sacrifice, and in fact, the "mother of all sacrifices." He is the sacrificial "lamb of God who takes away the sin of the world,"[3] whose slain carcass sufficiently and finally satisfies God's desire to be sacrificed to. Because Jesus' crucifixion has

2. Again, bad behaviors such as the overburning of fossil fuels, the mindless manufacturing of toxic waste materials, and agricultural practices geared only to the short-term are not *tov*. These are sin. Such practices are causing a troubling rise in average oceanic and atmospheric temperatures, rises that will trigger ever more non-*tov* weather and drought extremes, increases in insect populations, and new infectious disease outbreaks.

3. This phrase from John 1:29 is included in the Sunday liturgies of many Christian churches.

now satisfied God "once for all" (Rom 6:10 NRSV), henceforth, no more sacrifices are required. "Jesus did it; he died for the sins of the world and he died for me." Christians can now say, "If I believe this, and trust that the sacrificial system is now fulfilled and ended, I am saved."

I suggest that the sacrificial system was always a Cain concoction. It fit very well into Cain's retributive worldview. Projecting it onto God provided the requisite religious cover. But beyond this, it also had a ripple effect which contributed to additional harmful cultural values and practices. For example, by only making sacrifices presented by males worthy of God's acceptance, this system helped foster the sin of patriarchy. Think of the damage to girls and women (as well as to boys and men) the fabrication of patriarchy has perpetrated down through the ages. Also, "blemished" persons/animals/grains were considered unworthy. One wonders how significantly such thinking has contributed to the indifference, negative attitudes, and even discriminatory acts toward persons with disfigurements and disabilities that is common in many Cain societies. Consider these guidelines in the book of Leviticus:

> The LORD spoke to Moses, saying, "Speak to Aaron and say, 'No one of your offspring throughout their generations who has a *blemish* may approach to offer the food of his God. For no one who has a blemish shall draw near, one who is *blind* or *lame,* or one who has a *mutilated face* or a *limb too long,* or one who has a *broken foot* or a *broken hand,* or a *hunched back,* or a *dwarf,* or a man with a *blemish in his eyes* or an *itching disease* or *scabs* or *crushed testicles.*" (Lev 21:16–20, italics added NRSV)

It is not hard to see how numerous slights and oppressions would find acceptance under the guise of this "religious" practice.

- *Substitution theory of the atonement:* This common theory portrays God as seething with anger at humanity's sin. God's wrath needs to be expelled somewhere. In Cain's worldview, retributive justice requires that sin be punished. Somebody must pay. Thankfully, in grace, God provides a substitute—his son—and transmits this built-up fury onto a surrogate. Jesus of Nazareth becomes the substitutionary scapegoat upon whom the Deity vents divine anger. "Jesus died for me," Christians can now say. "I deserved the punishment, but Jesus took the hit. If I believe and trust this, I am saved."

This theory is another Cain fabrication, in my view. It not only suggests that God is incapable of self-control when it comes to anger, but that God is like an abusive father figure who needs to have somebody pained in order to feel better. Somebody must pay.

- *Ransom theory of the atonement:* This theory envisions a kidnapping. Satan abducts humanity, holds humanity hostage, and demands a ransom for humanity's safe release and return. Because God loves us so much, God agrees to the transaction and hands the payment (the crucified carcass of Jesus) over to Satan in a briefcase (tomb) as a saving payoff. Satan honors the deal and God gets humanity back. "Jesus paid the price; Jesus died for me," Christians can now say. "If I believe this, I am saved."

Yes, another Cain concoction. I cannot imagine the Deity agreeing to a deal like this with any Satan figure.

- *Super-sufferer theory of the atonement:* This theory argues that God was impressed with the no-holds-barred devotion of Jesus and his willingness to undergo painful rejection and suffering. Jesus was even willing to give up his young life. This monumental display of faithfulness earned him a treasury of merit. This is the basic theology of Mel Gibson's violence-laden 2005 movie, *The Passion of the Christ.* Walter Wink, in his book *The Powers That Be,* calls this "the myth of redemptive violence."[4] This culturally ingrained myth believes that violence and suffering need to happen for goodness to come. Life is combat, violence saves, suffering is required, and war brings peace. According to this atonement theory, it is Jesus' suffering that earns God's grace and favor and makes God want to

---

4. Wink, *Powers That Be,* 42.

save humans "for Jesus' sake." Christians who believe this and are willing to also suffer are now saved.

All four of these atonement theories can be found in the Bible. They are alive and well in the theologies of many church denominations today, and in Cain-ism's militaristic culture. The problem with all these theories is this: they are grounded in retribution. Some require punishment. Others demand payoffs to avoid punishment. Jesus helps humans escape the punishment, but someone (Jesus) must take the fall. My question is this: How do these theories fit with the notion of a loving and forgiving God? If grace must be merited— that is, earned (by anyone, including Jesus)—is it really grace?

These traditional atonement theories focus on Jesus' death. They basically argue that Jesus came to die. His death is the heart of the matter. This is the purpose of his incarnation and ministry.

The church's main creeds reinforce this theology. Notice how the Apostles' Creed (circa 390 CE) jumps immediately in one giant leap from "born of the virgin Mary" to "suffered under Pontius Pilate, was crucified, died, and was buried." The Nicene Creed (325 CE) does the same. Think of the significance of what is skipped— namely, thirty-three years of living on Earth as Abel of Nazareth. The church leaders who composed the creeds had other concerns on their minds relative to their time and place. These concerns are worthy of our appreciation and respect. But the final product tellingly omits Jesus' healings, teachings, exorcisms, and conflicts with the powers and principalities of culture and country and religion. It avoids his unwillingness to employ violence to solve problems ("those who live by the sword [or gun or missile] die by the sword"[5]). It overlooks his love for the stranger, outcast, alien, and enemy. It pushes to the side the way he perceptively beheld the "birds of the air and lilies of the field."[6] In short, neither historic creed picks up on Jesus' tenacious refusal to affirm or adopt Cain's ways.[7]

5. See Matt 26:52.
6. See Matt 6:26–29.
7. In like manner, we note how both creeds leap immediately from the

So, what then does the cross mean? Is there an alternative understanding to the assumptions mentioned above?

Of course, Jesus needed to die in order to be resurrected. You cannot have one without the other. Also, we can appreciate how the experience of suffering, rejection, torture, and death widened the Creator's solidarity with creation (including humanity), which suffers so intensely and viscerally from the effects of Cain's mutiny. The cross likewise gave humanity a peek into the heart of God's love for the world.

But what else does the fuller Jesus event teach us?

Here is an alternative to consider: God's story of Jesus shows God's preference for the Abel way. While Abel's narrative and Abel's rich storehouse of wisdom will always provoke violent reactivity in Cain, and even might get a person killed (crucified), still the LORD had "regard for Abel and his offering, but for Cain and his offering he had no regard" (Gen 4:5 NRSV). Abel living is near and dear to the heart of God.

Also, while Jesus' death could have occurred in a variety of ways, the Roman Empire's brutal cross death does serve a unique purpose in *mirroring* back to us what our strutting Cain-ism actually looks like. What does it look like? It looks like the Creator's goodness in human form and in living color rejected, abused, tortured, humiliated, lynched, and crucified by me and mine. Yes, Cain-ism is this ugly. Cain's shattering of sacred relationship with neighbor, Nature, the inner soul, and God cannot be whitewashed or rationalized away. It is plunderous. It is foul. It is inexcusable.

But along with *mirror*, the cross also serves as a *window*. The hanging Abel Christ also provides my species with a holy glimpse into the broken heart of God. It delivers a deep peek into the immense love of God for all Creation, including humans, including Abel, and surprisingly, even including Cain. The cross event boldly proclaims: "God loves this world, and God will not give up on it." Even when Cain rises up to defeat Abel of Nazareth and crows in triumph, Easter

---

creation of the universe (Article 1) to the birth of Jesus (Article 2). This leaves out 13.8 billion years of God's activity and engagement, including 3.8 billion years of Earth life. It also omits most of humanity's 300,000-year history. In my view, new creeds should be written to reflect God's larger story.

demonstrates unmistakably that Cain-ism's killing machines do not have ultimate power over Jesus or over those who follow him. Jesus is resurrected. He is risen. He is alive then and today. His resurrected presence will continue to display God's love every day and in every way, so that "neither death, nor life, nor angels, nor rulers, nor things present, nor things to come, nor powers, nor height, nor depth, nor anything else in all creation, will be able to separate us from the love of God in Christ Jesus our Lord" (Rom 8:37–39 NRSV).

So, it must be stated clearly and boldly that Jesus did not come to die. Rather, he came to live. He wasn't born for the purpose of dying a "cross death" that would somehow satisfy God's supposed need for a sacrifice. His carcass was not a requisite scapegoat or ransom payment. His suffering was not a test that, if passed, would earn God's favor. His death was inevitable, certainly, as it is for all creatures. Life and death are part and parcel within the realm of God's *tov* world. But dying on a cross was not the objective. Instead, Jesus came to live. He came to live a certain way, the Abel way, and to call the rest of his species to follow him into God's more favorable, sustainable, beloved, and excellent way. Did Jesus know Abel living might get him killed? Probably. It had not taken him long to figure out Cain-ism's values, worldviews, and behaviors, and their vulgar consequences. But he did not come to die a "cross death." Rather, he came to live a "cross life."

Did Jesus' resurrection overcome death? No. Death is still part and parcel of God's *tov* world. All mortal creatures, including humans, will live for a time and then croak. What Jesus did do, however, is overcome perishing. What is perishing? Perishing is what happens when people break sacred relationships with neighbor, with Nature, with our inner spirits/souls/selves, and with God. The good news (gospel) is that the risen Christ declares forgiveness for this inexcusable brokenness. And the good news is that Jesus the living Christ calls us daily to go with him into places of healing and relationship restoration.

In the big picture, death is not the problem. Perishing is. So, a person can be walking around town today but still be perishing. And someone could have died this morning and not be perishing at all.

༄

Reflection Questions

1. What in your mind is the allure of Cain-ism? Why do so many people prefer it to the wisdom of Abel?
2. Are doctrines such as original sin simply misunderstood and therefore misused, or do they need to be replaced?
3. Which atonement theory is most prevalent in your tradition?
4. What are the implications of the statement "Jesus didn't come to die a cross death, but to live a cross life (one that got him killed)"? What is refreshing about this take? What is hard to swallow?

PART FOUR

The Way Forward

Chapter 15

Abel Christianity

MY GOAL IN THIS book has been to reframe and recast Christianity's version of God's story of life and God's story of Jesus. The ideologies of human-ism which I have outlined need to be set aside and readily replaced by God's larger narrative, or what I am calling "Abel Christianity." This larger narrative draws from both Nature and the Bible. Both are "earthen vessels" (2 Cor 4:7 RSV) conveying God's voice, regard, and transformative message. Both "scriptures" inform, correct, enhance, mend, and amend one another.

The Christian community has played a significant role in humanity's accumulative ecological irresponsibility. Narratives of "dominion-ism" and "subduing the earth" have been widely embraced and sanctified as righteous. They need to be discarded. We humans are not exceptional as a species, nor are we the primary (primate) or wise ones (*Homo sapiens*). We certainly are not meant to be in charge. All ecosystems and species diversities of God's entire Creation constitute God's beloved and exceptional household. With grateful hearts, we get to be residents in this household too. God's expectation is that we be honorable housemates, not possessors or landlords or vendors. A deeper understanding of God's primary and secondary missions is needed.

As I have suggested, early in Christian history, Western civilization's ubiquitous narrative of human-ism achieved remarkable success by overtaking the Christian movement too. Western

Christianity was usurped and its truth was domesticated. Abel of Nazareth (Jesus) ended up being replaced by Cain of Nazareth (less than Jesus). How did this happen?

The Roman emperor Constantine (272–337 CE) played a pivotal role in this tragic triumph. After becoming a "Christian," Constantine established Christianity as the official religion of the Empire and began marginalizing those who would not acquiesce. He militarized the faith, in effect transforming the Prince of Peace into a sanctifier of warfare and conquest. He "orthodoxified" the wildness of the faith in pursuit of theological and political hegemony. And he blessed Cain's broad-gauge assault on Nature.

In many regions of the Empire, forests were home to numerous creatures. Trees provided homesteads and resources for countless animals, including humans. Within these forests, humans found fuel for heating and cooking, timber for building shelter, planks for watercraft, and lumber for tools like spinning wheels and wine presses. The forest ecosystem was central to the lives of its inhabitants, affecting everything from climate to poetry, trade to survival.

Over time, in hundreds of Abel cultures, sacred stories involving forests emerged. There were forest legends, mythological forest creatures, and religious rites involving tree spirits, offerings, healings, and prayers. As the Cain religion of Constantine took over the playing field, indigenous, forest-related beliefs and rituals came to be labeled "pagan." The people who held these beliefs, as well as the forest itself, came to be seen as under the spell of darkness, tainted by apparitions and demons, and backed by superstitious myths. For many, then, it seemed reasonable to conclude that it was a Christian duty to clear the forest, cut down the trees, push back the chaos, tame Nature, and make space and place for the clear and pure light of Christian civilization to break forth across the land. By 1600 CE, Europe had gone from a 95 percent forest covering to approximately 20 percent. Surely Abel engaged in forest husbandry as needed. But as Christianity blended with Cain-ism, axing trees became a hallowed mission (and lucrative industry) serving to sanctify Cain's already-significant war against God's garden.

In acting out this disfigured narrative, Christians have served as agents of harm in Cain-ism's victories over Nature and over Abel.

The question is: Can this damaging narrative be replaced before it is too late?

☙

Jonathan Wilson-Hartgrove's recent book *Reconstructing the Gospel: Finding Freedom from Slaveholder Religion* provides a helpful insight into a needed healing process. According to Wilson-Hartgrove, those of us who are North Americans have inherited a "slaveholder religion"—that is, a slavery system's version of the Christian gospel. What he means by this is that Christians today have received from our forebearers a version of Christian faith that for generations made peace with kidnapping Africans, enslaving Africans, slave-trading Africans, slave-breeding Africans, and slave-working Africans. There were actually church attenders who were proud enslavers, and preachers who were blind to the contradictions. As mentioned earlier, in postbellum America this false version of the Christian faith continued as Whites created and/or accommodated Black Codes and Jim Crow laws. They promoted or uncritically accepted White versions of history, filled church buildings with White-Jesus symbolism, tolerated all-White police squads/juries/judgeships, allowed the discounting of Black witnesses in favor of White witnesses in trials, kept quiet about the double-standard mass incarceration of Blacks, overlooked thousands of lynchings by mobs of White citizens,[1] promoted or turned a blind eye to Black voter suppression and sabotage, safeguarded White rule, and generally coexisted with persistent structures of racism. White Christians have even repeatedly voted for and supported racist sheriffs, judges, legislators, governors, and presidents, believing that this is not a disqualifying character trait.[2]

This slaveholder religion, according to Wilson-Hartgrove, has distorted our understanding of God's story of life and God's story

1. The recently opened National Lynching Memorial and Museum in Montgomery, Alabama revisits decades of terrorism against Black citizens committed by White citizens. See https://museumandmemorial.eji.org/.

2. After fifteen years (1978–93) of opposing the establishment of a federal holiday honoring Martin Luther King Jr., Cain finally yielded grudgingly, but only after figuring out a way to usurp the civil rights movement by using the rhetoric of "look how far we've come" to thwart any further dismantling of White rule.

of Jesus. In fact, we have inherited a distorted Christian "gospel" which, he argues, is in need of holy reconstruction. Hence the title of his book: *Reconstructing the Gospel: Finding Freedom from Slaveholder Religion.*

Unsurprisingly, biblical interpretation has been significantly warped on many levels by the norms of Cain-ism. There are numerous examples to be considered, but here is one. It involves a well-known and often-preached "stewardship" parable known as the "Parable of the Talents" (Matt 25:14–29 NRSV; cf. Luke 19:11–27).[3] The parable is often explained this way:

> A slaveholder entrusts a portion of his wealth/property (talents) to three slaves. One receives five talents, another two talents, and the third one talent, "each according to his ability." The enslaving master goes on a journey. While away, the slave with five talents doubles the master's holdings through work and investing. The slave with two talents does the same. However, the third slave digs a hole in the ground and buries his one talent. No investing, no trading, no increase. When the master returns to settle accounts, the slave with five talents hands over ten. The slave with two talents hands over four. But the slave with one talent hands back just the original one.
>
> Interpreters and preachers are taught to look for Jesus or God (or righteousness) in a parable. In traditional interpretations, the master is usually seen as this Christ figure. Following this line of thinking, the two slaves who double the master's holdings are deemed "good and trustworthy." As a reward, they are "put in charge of many things" and allowed to "enter into the joy of their master." Slave #3, on the other hand, is the bad guy, "wicked and lazy." The upshot in this supposed stewardship sermon is that we should be like the first two slaves who model Christian industry and stewardship, and not like the third who wastes what God bestows.

Here is a question I have asked myself: Why would I think that the slaveholder is the Jesus or God figure, the righteous one? A slaveholder is a thief. A slaveholder is an I-centered (and often

3. All quotes used in this section are from Matt 25:14–29 NRSV.

murderous) gangster who steals the labor, livelihood, and very lives of others. Is this what Jesus desires in his followers? What vestiges of "slaveholder religion," to use Wilson-Hartgrove's term, are in me? Why would I so mindlessly think and preach in this way? (Yes, I have preached this as a stewardship sermon many times, never thinking as a privileged White man how someone with the boot of injustice on their necks might read it.)

So, if the slaveholder is not the Jesus figure in the parable, where might we find Jesus? Hmm. In the life of the third slave? This guy knows quite well that the master is dishonorable. (If he were honorable, he would stop enslaving others, would repay everyone for every hour of work stolen and injustice imposed, and would put himself in prison for the rest of his life for crimes against creation, humanity, and God.)

Furthermore, this third slave knows better than anyone that the slaveholder is "a harsh man," as well as a crook who "reaps where he does not sow, and gathers where he does not scatter seed" (an admirable character trait in Cain-ism's distorted value system). This third slave also knows all too well that in the unjust structures of the world, "those who already have abundance" get more, and "from those who have nothing, even what they have will be taken away."

Could it be that the pastoral word of God and the prophetic word of God in this parable are that Jesus is the subversive one, the "worthless slave" who resists, undermines, sabotages, and refuses to be silent or to honor the slaveholder's tyranny . . . who is then cast out into "outer darkness" along with all the others who have been thrown away by the powers and principalities of Cain's world? Could it be that the true Jesus is a savior who chooses to dwell with the marginalized and discarded, and who weeps in solidarity with those for whom there is far too much "weeping and gnashing of teeth"?

Furthermore, could it also be that the writer, Matthew, did not quite "get" the meaning of Jesus' parable either? When we are careful to look for both the pastoral word of God and the prophetic word of God in every text, but especially in the whole and heart of Scripture, it jolts our easy interpretations. It turns upside down and inside out how we read the Bible.

ॐ

Christian ethicist and theologian Dr. Larry Rasmussen points out that we mistakenly also apply the same "master-slave" scaffolding when it comes to ecology. In his wonderful book *Earth-Honoring Faith: Religious Ethics in a New Key,* Rasmussen argues that much of humanity regards humans as masters who are put on Earth to control and exploit Nature. Similar to human-slavery systems, Nature here is considered "property to be bought, sold, and used in keeping with what is deemed necessary, desirable, and responsible on the part of the slaveholder."[4] Also, analogous to human-slavery systems, in this master-slave ecology ethic, some people imagine it is possible to be "nicer" or "more honorable" masters. This is a delusion. While current ecologically responsible practices by some Cains are certainly better than nothing—including recycling, composting, organic gardening, conserving energy, converting to renewables, water harvesting, sponsoring roadside cleanups, and trying not to purchase goods and services that are overtly harmful—these efforts will always be trumped by the more far-reaching forces of narrative. In fact, *any* narrative or worldview that positions the species *Homo sapiens* as separate from, superior to, the reason for, and the rulers of God's household will *always* override not only Nature and Abel, but also any attempt by Cain to be a nicer master.

Reversing the tide away from Cain's gloomy leitmotif toward the artful sway of Abel's decency will involve moving one's goals and desires away from Taker-ism toward Leaver-ism; from lifting up Pharaoh in favor of honoring Moses; from false prophets to truth-telling prophets; from denial to lament; from terror to grace; from Jabba the Hutt (a grotesque, over-consuming/over-polluting creature in the film *Star Wars,* also known as Pizza the Hutt in the Mel Brooks spoof called *Spaceballs*) to Jesus; from dominion thinking to belonging; from control to kinship; from harming the Earth to biomass increase and sustainability.

In summary, the heart of this book is this: the Narrative must change.

---

4. Rasmussen, *Earth-Honoring Faith,* 100.

As I have suggested in these pages, God's voice and word is to be found in two scriptures—Nature and Bible. All ecosystems and species throughout the universe, including humans, "read" the first; only humans read the second. I have also suggested that bearing an orientation to both is indispensable for faithful Christian living.

I believe that for us moderns, the way into God's voice and word in Nature is through studies in Nature's natural sciences—physics, astronomy, geology, evolutionary biology, paleoanthropology, forestry, zoology, ecology, etc. This is because in our time we have mostly lost the capacity for a more intuitive and visceral access possessed by other species, as well as by our own human ancestors and predecessor species. They live in kinship within the multilayered ecosystems and species diversities of Nature. We live separate from Nature. They know intuitively in their day-to-day livelihood so much more than our modern lifestyle can ever reveal.

It is true that many people today enjoy spending time hiking in the wild, gardening, sunset gazing and stargazing, visiting our national parks, camping, fishing and hunting for food, scuba diving or skydiving, canoeing or sailing, rock climbing or horseback riding. I also do many of these activities. However, while important, really this is just dabbling. On a more fundamental level, because of our lifestyles, we moderns have become "insentiently hampered." We no longer have the visceral and experiential intelligence and wisdom embodied in other species that our human forebears were able to share. We are living "outside of Eden."

This is why I am suggesting that for us moderns, the way into the ponderous wonders and holy voice of God's scriptures in Nature may be through Nature's natural sciences. It is not about returning to the past; it is about returning to the present, to what is right in front of our noses, only at a deeper level. On this score I especially commend to you the recent 2020 Craig Foster documentary film on Netflix entitled *My Octopus Teacher*, as well Joe Hutto's 2014 book entitled *Touching the Wild* and anything by the renowned writer and filmmaker David Attenborough.[5] In my view, Foster, Hutto, and Attenborough are Abel natural scientists.

Nature and Bible. In his wonderful book *Celebrating Nature by Faith*, Paul Santmire aptly describes the biblical testimony as centralizing and even elevating the species *Homo sapiens*.[6] If we read the Bible alone, this conclusion is reasonable. But if we accompany God's voice and word in the scriptures of the Bible with God's voice and word in the scriptures of Nature, we gain a perspective that is much larger, longer, worldview altering, and, I believe, more theologically astute. Humans are a recently arrived species. We are tiny—one among many. God's creating and creative partnership with atoms and bacteria is actually more essential to life than any potential partnership with humans. The world does not need us. It has thrived throughout most of its history without our presence. Human history is part of the story, certainly. But God's story is far larger and much more all-embracing.

Also, Santmire correctly describes the biblical testimony regarding eschatology. Creation, according to the Bible, was begun by God but is unfinished. Since the disobedience of Adam and Eve, it is even fundamentally broken. Hence, creation is moving forward toward something. It is evolving toward a future consummation, an omega point (to use Teilhard de Chardin's term) of fulfilment and/or ending. God's story in history is patiently but purposefully pursuing a final culmination characterized by a return to an Eden paradise. Notably, this is not just for humans, but for all of Nature. The prophet Isaiah even anticipates a time when the "wolf shall live with the lamb, the leopard shall lie down with the kid, the calf and the lion and the fatling together, and a little child shall lead them" (Isa 11:6 NRSV). There will be a new and improved reality where "the cow and the bear shall graze, their young shall lie down together; and the lion shall eat straw like the ox. The nursing child

---

5. See Bibliography.

6. Santmire, *Celebrating Nature by Faith*, 12-20.

shall play over the hole of the asp, and the weaned child shall put its hand on the adder's den" (11:7–8 NRSV).

God's voice in the natural sciences tempers this biblical view. While there may be occasions when a wolf will wantonly slay a lamb even though she does not really need the lamb for sustenance, overall, the daily activity of seeking food provisions is not a bad thing. It is not behavior that needs correction or healing. It is *tov*. It is good. It is the way God made the world.

Furthermore, it is true that five billion years from now the Sun may run out of hydrogen and transform into something else. And it is true that the accelerating expansion of the universe seems slated to cease some trillions of years into the future, and the universe itself to eventually even die out. Also, human misbehavior by means of ecological irresponsibility or a nuclear-war holocaust could indeed make Earth's biosphere mostly uninhabitable, wiping out our species and many others. But does it really seem plausible that God would be planning to bring an apocalyptic end to such an ancient, vast, and beloved wonder, as some writers in the Bible seem to teach?

Christians have much to learn from Nature's natural sciences regarding God's story. In fact, I believe that if we can become better schooled in the expansive depths of Article 1 of our Creeds (God as Creator), our interactions with Article 2 (Jesus) and Article 3 (Holy Spirit) will have the potential to be less anemic and more wholesome also.

Could this additionally be a two-way street? Might a mended and amended Christian faith also have something to share with the natural sciences? It is indeed worldview altering to understand that a loving God undergirds all that is, seen and unseen. Such a perspective has the potential to countenance Nature with an even more profound value, integrity, and purpose. It can even affect how humans, including natural scientists, live in this world. Will their guiding narrative in daily life, in the laboratory, in studies out in the field, and in product development be grounded in Abel's values, worldview, and behavior, or in Cain-ism?

ॐ

I intended initially to title this final chapter "What Next?" or "What Do We Do Now?" or even—borrowing from Dr. Martin Luther King Jr.'s transformational book—"Where Do We Go From Here?" Upon further reflection, I decided these steps are premature. A desire to merely tweak or even to rush toward quick remedies may only serve to truncate a necessary disquiet in favor of restoring comfortableness. Forging ahead in the wrong direction is not making headway. Cain-ism's narrative is inextricably woven into the fabric and chemistry of our psyche, mythmaking, precedents, family systems, theological constructions, households, institutions, religious practices, news reporting, educational systems, humor (what is funny and what is not), and everyday habits. This needs to be dealt with. Remnants of Abel do exist in parts of the world, especially within some indigenous populations, and may even be locked away in some deep crevices of Cain's soul. But for the most part, Cain-ism rules our species. Even the university system where I have served as campus pastor is a Cain institution. Its primary job is to train Cain students on how to be successful Cains in a Cain world (although thankfully, there are always a few Abel professors and students who find a way to transcend the system and move beyond smartness in their careers and daily lives into the realms of intelligence, wisdom, and ethics).[7]

We must ask ourselves what forces keep everyone (including Christians) from seeing this, and why for so long? The answer is that Cain-ism's effectiveness has left all of us (myself included):

- deeply socialized

- comfortable with the benefits the system provides

- indifferent to those who do not benefit

- sheltered from seeing the ecological underbelly of our lifestyle

- shielded from a more truthful view of history (so brilliantly analyzed by Isabel Wilkerson[8])

7. Again, in using the Abel and Cain characters, I am not offering a scholarly exegesis of their story sequence in Gen 4:1–16. Rather, it is a template. I find this to be a helpful way of thinking about two different narratives and the implications of living out of one narrative as opposed to the other.

8. Wilkerson, *Caste.*

- defensive

- expert at chasing diversions

- fragile when challenged (especially White people, as so brilliantly analyzed by Robin DiAngelo[9])

- buttressed by a catalogue of false myths that render us unscathed in any situation

- deaf to God's "voice" in both scriptures (Nature and Bible)

- under the spell of master-slave religion

- empty inside, but in hot pursuit of Cain-ism's titillating fillers

- hooked on false equilibrium and the need to feel safe and comfortable

- addicted to the future as a way of avoiding or minimizing past and present realities

- and finally, as stated multiple times throughout this book, disconnected from experiencing challenging, transformative, and refreshing pools of sacred relationship with neighbor, Nature, our inner soul/spirit/self, and God.

These forces have combined into an overarching narrative that blinds most of humanity from the cruel wake of Cain's dominionism, and our own inexorable participation in it. While it is possible to be both Cain and Abel in our behavior (in fact it is likely, myself included), it is not possible to be both Cain and Abel in our narrative. Transforming the narrative is where our energies must be applied, especially in Western Christianity and Western civilization.[10]

9. DiAngelo, *White Fragility*.

10. Cain-ism's narrative is an ideology, not a philosophy or theology. Because philosophies and theologies are open to challenge and new learnings, they tend to mature over time and can be helpful guides for human living. Ideologies, on the other hand, are a bottleneck. An ideology only lets in information and truths that pre-fit the ideology—or it frames incoming information in a way that pre-fits established ideological slots. Being guided by philosophy and theology is good. Being guided by an ideology is maturity-stunting. This is why a radio personality like Rush Limbaugh (1951–2021) could declare that he was able to do what he does with "half my brain tied behind my back." Indeed, the whole brain (and heart and soul) was not being used. Of course,

❧

In the Gospel of John, Jesus the Christ declares, "If you continue in my word, you are truly my disciples; and you will know the truth, and the truth will make you free" (John 8:31 NRSV). In the version of Christian faith and life I am proposing, this word and voice of God springs forth throughout the scriptures of Nature and Bible. Christians and others need to be astutely attentive to both. Concerning ecology and the Bible, it is not so much that we need to better lift up what certain Bible passages say about creation and ecology. Rather, we need an ecology- and theology-*grounded* Christian faith in order to understand what the Bible has to say about anything, including the story of Israel and of Jesus. It is a matter of going deep into this well of blessing, and then having the courage to truly hear, live, and share what we find.

❧

Reflection Questions

1. Discuss the implications of Constantine's domestication of Christianity, especially its relation to "clearing the forest."
2. How on target is Wilson-Hartgrove's assertion that the Christian gospel itself needs reconstruction?
3. Is my reinterpretation of the "Parable of the Talents" valid?
4. Discuss Larry Rasmussen's assertion that the "master-slave" ideology vis à vis Nature has also overtaken Christian theology.
5. Compare Isaiah's vision of wolves and lambs hanging out together in the future with the concept of *tov*.
6. Do you think God is planning to bring the universe to an end?
7. Discuss the distinctions made between philosophies and theologies (positive influences) and an ideology (a negative influence).
8. I have argued that "Narrative" is key. To what extent do you agree and disagree?

Cain-ism will always try to argue that Abel living is an ideology too. But this is not the case. Abel living is a philosophy, theology, and practice that is open to what life is teaching. It is open to mending and amendment.

Epilogue

I HAVE DISCLOSED ON these pages an ongoing faith journey. It is tactile and window opening to me, receptive to both God's sunlight and heavy rain. God grants one life to live. I tremble when I think about any creature, including of the human kind, whose presence and contribution has been needlessly disregarded or snuffed out inexcusably early. It saddens me even more when this snuffing has sometimes been carried out by Christians.

Some presume that the Christian story and grace's wondrous implications were fully discerned and settled upon during a former period of history, perhaps by those early first-century Christians. "If we could just recover a more genuine past, then all or most would be fine," this view reasons. My view is that we are not there yet. Christians and others have not yet grasped the insinuations and peregrinations of God's pastoral and prophetic story of life and God's pastoral and prophetic story of Jesus—let alone truly lived them. There is much yet to learn and little time. Or maybe a long time; I do not know.

I continue to find my life, by God's grace, regenerative. On most mornings I chirp internally like the birds bursting with joy. My earthiness in body and soul continues to be a gift, and this book's testament to the Christian community and beyond has been shared with deep regard. May God continue to work transformation in me and in the whole human family.

Ron Rude

Bibliography

Aldersey-Williams, Hugh. *Periodic Tales: A Cultural History of the Elements, from Arsenic to Zinc.* New York: HarperCollins, 2011.

Alexander VI. *Inter caetera.* In *European Treaties bearing on the History of the United States and its Dependencies to 1648,* edited by Frances Gardiner Davenport, editor, 75–78. Washington, DC: Carnegie Institution of Washington, 1917.

Angier, Natalie. *The Canon: A Whirligig Tour of the Beautiful Basics of Science.* Boston: Houghton Mifflin, 2007.

Attenborough, David. *A Life on Our Planet: My Witness Statement and a Vision for the Future.* New York: Grand Central, 2020.

Bacon, Francis. *Of the Wisdom of the Ancients.* In *The Works of Francis Bacon,* edited by James Spedding et al. London: Longman, 1857–1870; Bartleby. com, 2010. www.bartleby.com/82/.

Barber, William J., and Jonathan Wilson-Hartgrove. *The Third Reconstruction: How a Moral Movement is Overcoming the Politics of Division and Fear.* Boston, MA: Beacon, 2016.

Barber, William J., et al. *Revive Us Again: Vision and Action in Moral Organizing.* Boston: Beacon, 2018.

Bloomquist, Karen L., et al., eds. *Radicalizing Reformation: North American Perspectives.* Zürich, Switzerland: LIT Verlag, 2016.

Bonhoeffer, Dietrich. *The Cost of Discipleship,* 2nd ed. New York: MacMillian, 1959.

Bornkamm, Heinrich. *Luther's World of Thought.* Translated by Martin H. Bertram. St. Louis: Concordia, 1958.

Boss, Gayle. *Wild Hope: Stories for Lent from the Vanishing.* Brewster, MA: Paraclete, 2020.

Brueggemann, Walter. *Journey to the Common Good.* Louisville, KY: Westminster John Knox, 2010.

———. *The Prophetic Imagination,* 2nd ed. Minneapolis: Fortress, 2001.

Bryson, Bill. *A Short History of Nearly Everything.* New York: Broadway, 2003.

Carson, Rachel. *Silent Spring.* New York: Houghton Mifflin, 1962.

Chernow, Ron. *Alexander Hamilton.* New York: Penguin, 2004.

Coyne, Jerry A. *Why Evolution is True*. New York: Penguin Group, 2009.

Dahill, Lisa E., and James B. Martin-Schramm, eds. *Eco-Reformation: Grace and Hope for a Planet in Peril*. Eugene, OR: Wipf and Stock, 2016.

"A Declaration of the Causes Which Impel the State of Texas to Secede from the Federal Union." In *Journal of the Secession Convention of Texas 1861*, edited by Ernest William Winkler, 61–65. Austin: Texas Library and Historical Commission, 1912. tsl.texas.gov/ref/abouttx/secession/2feb1861.html.

De Waal, Frans. *Are We Smart Enough to Know How Smart Animals Are?* New York: W. W. Norton & Company, 2016.

DiAngelo, Robin. *White Fragility: Why It's So Hard for White People to Talk About Racism*. Boston: Beacon, 2018.

Drew, Liam. *I, Mammal: The Story of What Makes Us Mammals*. London: Bloomsbury Sigma, 2017.

Egan, Timothy. *The Good Rain: Across Time and Terrain in the Pacific Northwest*. New York: Vintage, 1990.

Eisler, Raine. *The Chalice and the Blade: Our History, Our Future*. San Francisco: Harper, 1988.

Erlander, Daniel. *Manna and Mercy: A Brief History of God's Unfolding Promise to Mend the Entire Universe*. Minneapolis: Augsburg Fortress, 1992.

Genoways, Ted. *This Blessed Earth: A Year in the Life of an American Family Farm*. New York: W. W. Norton & Company, 2018.

Gould, Stephen Jan, ed. *The Book of Life: An Illustrated History of the Evolution of Life on Earth*. New York: W. W. Norton & Company, 2001.

Gregersen, Niels Henrik. "Deep Incarnation: Why Evolutionary Continuity Matters in Christology." *Toronto Journal of Theology* 26.2 (2010) 173–88.

Groenfeldt, David. *Water Ethics: A Values Approach to Solving the Water Crisis*. New York: Routledge, 2013.

Gustafson, Scott W. *At the Altar of Wall Street: The Rituals, Myths, Theologies, Sacraments, and Mission of the Religion Known as the Modern Global Economy*. Grand Rapids: Wm. B. Eerdmans, 2015.

———. *Biblical Amnesia: A Forgotten Story of Redemption, Resistance, and Renewal*. West Conshohocken, PA: Infinity, 2004.

Harari, Yuval Noah. *Sapiens: A Brief History of Humankind*. New York: HarperCollins, 2015.

Haught, John F. *Responses to 101 Questions on God and Evolution*. New York: Paulist, 2001.

Hunter, T. Russell. "Making a Theist out of Darwin: Asa Gray's Post-Darwinian Natural Theology." *Science and Education* 21.7 (July 2012) 959–75.

Hutto, Joe. *Touching the Wild: Living with the Mule Deer of Dead Man Gulch*. New York: Skyhorse, 2016.

Impey, Chris. *How It Began: A Time-Traveler's Guide to the Universe*. New York: W. W. Norton & Company, 2012.

Jenkins, Martin, and Grahame Baker-Smith. *Life, the First Four Billion Years: The Story of Life from the Big Bang to the Evolution of Humans*. Somerville, MA: Candlewick, 2019.

Jones, Ellis. *The Better World Shopping Guide*. Gabriola Island, BC: New Society, 2018.

Kierkegaard, Søren. *The Sickness unto Death*. Princeton: Princeton University Press, 1941.

Lopez, Barry Holstun. *Of Wolves and Men*. New York: Charles Scriber & Sons, 1979.

Macy, Joanna, and Molly Brown. *Coming Back to Life: The Updated Guide to the Work That Connects*. Gabriola Island, BC: New Society, 2014.

Martínez, Antonio Marco. "Man is the Measure." *Antiquitatem—History of Greece and Rome* (blog). June 3, 2013. http://www.antiquitatem.com/en/plato-protagoras-philosophy-sophist/.

Marilyn. "You've Come a Long Way, Baby: Cigarette Ads of 1972." *Musings from Marilyn* (blog). August 9, 2016. https://blog.finnfemme.com/2016/08/youve-come-a-long-way-baby-cigarette-ads-of-1972/.

Massing, Michael. *Fatal Discord: Erasmus, Luther, and the Fight for the Western Mind*. New York: HarperCollins, 2018.

McDaniel, Jay. "Spirituality and Sustainability." *Conservation Biology* 15.6 (2002) 1461–64.

McDough, William, and Michael Braungart. *Cradle to Cradle: Remaking the Way We Make Things*. New York: North Point, 2002.

McFague, Sallie. *Super, Natural Christians: How We Should Love Nature*. Minneapolis: Augsburg, 1997.

McLaren, Brian D. *Faith after Doubt: Why Your Beliefs Stopped Working and What to Do about It*. New York: St. Martin's Essentials, 2021.

McPherson, James. *The War That Forged a Nation*. New York: Oxford University Press, 2015.

Meacham, Jon. *American Lion: Andrew Jackson in the White House*. New York: Random House, 2008.

———. *The Soul of America: The Battle for Our Better Angels*. New York: Random House, 2018.

"Mississippi Secession." National Park Service: US Department of the Interior. https://www.nps.gov/articles/ms-secession.htm.

Moe-Lobeda, Cynthia D. *Resisting Structural Evil: Love as Ecological-Economic Vocation*. Minneapolis: Fortress, 2013.

Mott Lacroix, Kelly, et al. *Roadmap for Considering Water for Arizona's Natural Areas*. Tucson, Arizona: Water Resources Research Center, University of Arizona, 2014. https://wrrc.arizona.edu/sites/wrrc.arizona.edu/files/attach ment/Roadmap_Complete_2014_1.pdf.

Nessan, Craig L. *Shalom Church: The Body of Christ as Ministering Community*. Minneapolis: Fortress, 2010.

Nicholas V. *Dum Diversas*. Tyler History. http://www.tylerhistory.org/2018/08 /27/1452-papal-bull-dum-diversas/.

———. *Romanus Pontifex*. In *European Treaties bearing on the History of the United States and its Dependencies to 1648*, edited by Frances Gardiner Davenport, 20–26. Washington, DC: Carnegie Institution of Washington,

1917. https://doctrineofdiscovery.org/the-bull-romanus-pontifex-nicholas
-v/.

Nilsen-Goodwin, Solveig. *What is the Way of the Wilderness? An Introduction to the Wilderness Way Community.* Des Moines, IA: Zion, 2016.

Obama, Barack. *A Promised Land.* New York: Crown, 2020.

Quinn, Daniel. *Beyond Civilization: Humanity's Next Great Adventure.* New York: Three Rivers, 1999.

————. *Ishmael: An Adventure of the Mind and Spirit.* New York: Bantam, 1992.

Raheb, Mitri, ed. *The Invention of History: A Century of Interplay between Theology and Politics in Palestine.* Bethlehem, West Bank: Diyar, 2011.

Rasmussen, Larry L. *Earth-Honoring Faith: Religious Ethics in a New Key.* New York: Oxford University Press, 2013.

Rhoads, David, ed. *Earth and Word: Classic Sermons on Saving the Planet.* New York: Continuum, 2007.

Rohr, Richard. *The Universal Christ: How a Forgotten Reality Can Change Everything We See, Hope for, and Believe.* New York: Convergent, 2019.

Rude, Ron. *Abel Emerging: A Reconsideration of the Christian Story for a Sustainable World.* Edina, MN: Beaver's Pond, 2010.

————. *(Re)considering Christianity: An Expedition of Faith Joining Science, Ancient Wisdom, and Sustainability.* Edina, MN: Beaver's Pond, 2012.

Sala, Enric. *The Nature of Nature: Why We Need the Wild.* Washington, DC: National Geographic, 2020.

Salatin, Joel. *The Marvelous Pigness of Pigs: Respecting and Caring for all God's Creation.* New York: Faith, 2016.

Sandford, Maggie Ryan. *Consider the Platypus: Evolution through Biology's Most Baffling Beasts.* New York: Black Dog & Leventhal, 2019.

Santmire, H. Paul. *Celebrating Nature by Faith.* Eugene, OR: Cascade, 2020.

Scharf, Caleb. *The Zoomable Universe: An Epic Tour through Cosmic Scale, from Almost Everything to Nearly Nothing.* New York: Scientific American, 2017.

Schrijver, Karel, and Iris Schrijver. *Living with the Stars: How the Human Body is Connected to the Life Cycles of Planets, Suns, Stars.* London: Oxford University Press, 2015.

Shubin, Neil. *Your Inner Fish: A Journey into the 3.5-Billion-Year History of the Human Body.* New York: Random, 2008.

Snyder, Timothy. *On Tyranny: Twenty Lessons from the Twentieth Century.* New York: Tim Dugan, 2016.

Stark, Peter. *Astoria: John Jacob Astor and Thomas Jefferson's Lost Pacific Empire: A Story of Wealth, Ambition, Survival.* New York: Harper Collins, 2014.

Stringer, Curtis, and Peter Andrews. *The Complete World of Human Evolution.* Devon, England: Thames & Hudson, 2005.

Stump, J. B., and Alan G. Padgett. *The Blackwell Companion to Science and Christianity.* Malden, MA: Blackwell, 2012.

Tattersall, Ian. *Masters of the Planet: The Search for Our Human Origins.* New York: Palgrave MacMillian, 2012.

Theoharis, Jeanie. *A More Beautiful and Terrible History: The Uses and Misuses of Civil Rights History.* Boston: Beacon, 2018.

Tillich, Paul. "The Meaning of Health." *Perspectives in Biology and Medicine* 5.1 (Autumn 1961) 92–100.

Trafzer, Clifford E., ed. *American Indians, American Presidents: A History.* New York: HarperCollins, 2009.

"The Treaty of Paris." *American Legends* (podcast). April 9, 2017. http://www.americanlegendspodcast.com/?p=68%20(in%20part%203.

Tutu, Desmond. *No Future without Forgiveness.* New York: Doubleday, 1999.

Tyson, Neil DeGrasse. *Astrophysics for People in a Hurry.* New York: W. W. Norton & Company, 2017.

———. *Cosmic Queries: StarTalk's Guide to Who We Are, How We Got Here, and Where We're Going.* Washington, DC: National Geographic, 2021.

———. *Star Talk: Everything You Ever Need to Know about Space Travel, Sci-fi, the Human Race, the Universe, and Beyond.* Washington, DC: National Geographic, 2016.

Wheelan, Joseph. *Mr. Adam's Last Crusade: John Quincy Adams's Extraordinary Post-presidential Life in Congress.* New York: PublicAffairs, 2009.

Wilkerson, Isabel. *Caste: The Origins of Our Discontents.* New York: Random House, 2020.

Wink, Walter. *The Powers That Be: Theology for a New Millennium.* New York: Galilee Doubleday, 1998.

Wilson, Joseph R. "Mutual Relation of Masters and Slaves as Taught in the Bible." http://www.civilwarcauses.org/revwilson.htm.

Wilson-Hartgrove, Jonathan. *Reconstructing the Gospel: Finding Freedom from Slaveholder Religion.* Downers Grove, IL: InterVarsity, 2018.

Wulf, Andrea. *The Invention of Nature: Alexander Von Humboldt's New World.* New York: Vintage, 2016.

Yong, Ed. *I Contain Multitudes: The Microbes within Us, and a Grander View of Life.* New York: Harper Collins, 2016.

Zamoyski, Adam. *Napoleon: A Life.* New York: Basic Books, 2018.

Zimmer, Carl. *A Planet of Viruses.* Chicago: University of Chicago, 2011.